PORT IS
LIFEBOATS
AN ILLUSTRATED HISTORY

Nicholas Leach and Bob Bulgin BEM

FOXGLOVE PUBLISHING

Bob Bulgin

Page 1: Port Isaac inshore lifeboat Copeland Bell (D-707). (Nicholas Leach)

First published 2016

Published by
Foxglove Publishing Ltd
Foxglove House, Shute Hill, Lichfield WS13 8DB

United Kingdom
Tel 01543 673594

ISBN 9781909540064

Typesetting/layout by Nicholas Leach/Foxglove
Publishing

Published with the generous support of TJ INK
(www.tjink.co.uk) and printed in Premier Colour
by TJ International (www.tjinternational.ltd.uk)
on Maiden Silk FSC 130gsm supplied by Vision
Paper & Board (0844 556 1800).

Contents

	Foreword by Commodore Jamie Miller CBE	7
	Acknowledgements	8
THE VILLAGE	Port Isaac: its history	9
1869 – 1887	The First Lifeboat	13
1887 – 1905	A second Richard and Sarah Lifeboat	21
1905 – 1933	The last pulling lifeboats	29
1967 – 1997	Inshore Lifeboats	47
ARTWORK	Port Isaac Paintings	102
	Appendices	110

A Pulling and Sailing Lifeboats 110
B Inshore Lifeboats 110
C Pulling lifeboat service summary 111
D Inshore lifeboat service summary 112
E Personnel summary 116
F Lifeboat station personnel 2016 117
G Lifeboat crew 118

All proceeds from the sale of this book will benefit the RNLI

The first Port Isaac lifeboat house, built in 1869 and used until 1927, is now a well known landmark in the village, situated high up on the east side of the small bay, and a reminder of the time when the lifeboat had to be hauled through the streets by numerous helpers. (Nicholas Leach)

Dedicated to all the crew members and committee of Port Isaac RNLI

Crew members Jon Wide, Damien Bolton, James Bolton, Sam Eaves and George Cleave on the beach heading back to the boathouse after taking the ILB out on a training exercise. (Nicholas Leach)

The Extra Crewman by Eric Stokes

You'll meet the boat's crew as they stop for a chat,
Playing darts in the Lion, swapping yarns on the Platt.
There's fifteen or more, some old hands, some new,
But always enough to make up a crew.

When the rockets go up, and the gulls rise and screech,
They'll stop in mid-sentence, and make for the beach.
Launched and away, oftimes it's calm,
They may be recalled, just another alarm.

But when the sea boils, force six or more blow,
It's left to the crew, they vote, and they go!
Someone's in trouble, no ifs and no buts,
Tramping round Lobber, three lads or a girl with guts.

Ask the folk of Penlee, the maroons double crack
Means you have to go out, not always come back.
Two hours or more, before they come in,
Sometimes exhausted, and soaked to the skin,

Wash down the boat, check fuel's okay.
It's not unknown, for three 'shouts' a day
A chalk board's updated, 336 lives saved,
A surfer or sailor escapes a sea grave.

Proud of their job, proud of success,
Proud to be helping someone in distress.
So pause if you see our D class afloat,
Ask God to go with them, there's room in the boat.

Foreword

O f a lifeboat Sir Winston Churchill once said: 'It drives on with a mercy which does not quail in the presence of death. It drives on as proof, a symbol, a testimony that man is created in the image of God and that valour and virtue have not perished in the British Race'. As a mariner who has been sunk twice during my Royal Naval career – I hasten to add far away from the RNLI's domain – I have a certain empathy with Sir Winston's words and throughout my seagoing life have always held our Royal National Lifeboat Institution in high esteem, not least the Port Isaac station where valued friends serve.

As Port Isaac RNLI nears its 150th year, the station has an interesting and worthwhile story to tell, both from a historic point of view and because of the everyday and gallant rescue work carried out by its voluntary crew members, past and present. The lifeboats have saved 336 lives and launched 644 times since the D class inshore lifeboat came into service in 1967, while much fine work is carried out behind the scenes by the Committee.

So it is indeed an honour and a great pleasure to endorse this fascinating and worthwhile record of the lifeboat at Port Isaac. My best wishes to all: mariners, residents and holidaymakers; may you enjoy fair winds and a safe passage on or off the shores of North Cornwall's beautiful coast, safe in the knowledge that the RNLI is just a short call away, with its volunteers at the ready twenty-four hours a day, 365 days of the year, as is your Royal Navy.

Commodore Jamie Miller CBE Royal Navy
Naval Regional Commander Wales and Western England

With courage, nothing is impossible – Sir William Hillary

Acknowledgements

Many people have assisted with this project to produce a comprehensive history of the Port Isaac lifeboat station, and we are very grateful to them all. In Port Isaac, thanks to those who have supplied photographs from private family collections and personal accounts of lifeboat rescues, and to those that have given freely of their time, advice, encouragement, and most importantly the generous gift to finance the publication. We particularly acknowledge the help and support of Nigel Millard; Mike Lavis; Nathan Williams at the RNLI's Film and Imaging Unit; Roger Aldham at the RNLI; papers of the late David Castle and the late Surgeon Commodore Baskerville OBE; the UK Hydrographic Office; Nathan Outlaw; Geoff Provis; John Harrop, who kindly supplied photos and old postcards; Paul Richards; the Pottery; Sharps Brewery; Old School House Hotel; Buttermilk Confections; PLC Media; Palace Printers; The Port Gaverne Hotel; The Big Swim; Wave Hunters; Wovina; and TJ International. The authors acknowledge the work of Grahame Farr and Cyril Noall, whose book *Wreck and Rescue Round the Cornish Coast I: The Story of the North Coast Lifeboats*, published in 1964, provided the basis for the history of the station's pulling and sailing lifeboats; the *Port Isaac Lifeboat Centenary Booklet* was also useful. The RNLI Heritage Team, notably Hayley Whiting and Joanna Bellis, facilitated research. Thanks also to the Secrets Gallery and the artists Barbara Hawkins, Les Henson, Caroline Cleave, Sian Fletcher, Ray Balkwill and Roy Ritchie, and the Frank McNichol Trust.

The authors

• **Nicholas Leach** has a long-standing interest in lifeboats and the lifeboat service. He has written many articles, books and papers on the subject, including a history of the origins of the lifeboat service; a comprehensive record of the RNLI's lifeboat stations in 1999, the organisation's 175th anniversary; RNLI Motor Lifeboats, a detailed history of the development of powered lifeboats; and numerous station histories, including ones covering the Cornish stations of Padstow, Sennen Cove and Fowey. He has visited all of the lifeboat stations in the UK and Ireland, past and present, and is Editor of Ships Monthly, the international shipping magazine.

• **Bob Bulgin BEM** has sailed extensively in traditional boats, both as crew and as skipper, and helped to establish fixed seat traditional rowing on the Thames as one of the founders of the first Thames Waterman's Cutters. He was a founder of a British Sub-Aqua Club and has dived extensively both in home waters and around the world, helping to establish the British Divers Marine Life Rescue operation in Cornwall. He has had a close relationship with Port Isaac RNLI for many years, as an active committee member for twenty years and Chairman for ten. He was awarded the British Empire Medal in 2014, is a Freeman of the City of London and the Company of Waterman and Lightermen of the River Thames, a Member of the Old Gaffers Association, and a Fellow of the Royal Geographical Society.

Port Isaac: its history

There are few references to Port Isaac before the sixteenth century. Its name, 'Portizick', as spelled in Carew's Survey of Cornwall of 1602, indicates the origin of the village: the name has no biblical connection, but is derived from the Cornish words meaning 'corn port'. Inside the western breakwater are relics of an older structure dating back to Henry VIII's time, from which corn, grown on farms of Endellion and St Minver, was exported. Exports of corn were followed, during Elizabeth I's reign, by slate, which was mined at Delabole's slate quarry, and Port Isaac's active harbour saw cargoes, including stone, timber and pottery, being loaded and unloaded. This industry continued until comparatively recent times at Port Gaverne, where the track used by the horse-drawn carts to reach the 'quay' on the east side of the bay is still known as 'cartway'. Coal was also imported at Port

An aerial view of the village of Port Isaac, as seen by an RNLI crew member when on exercise with a helicopter from 771 Squadron, RNAS Culdrose, looking east.

Two views of the small village of Port Isaac, with the houses and buildings clustered round the harbour. Port Isaac, set in an Area of Outstanding Natural Beauty, has been an attractive fishing village since the early fourteenth century, but the village centre dates from the eighteenth and nineteenth centuries, from a time when its prosperity was tied to local coastal freight and fishing. The small port handled cargoes of coal, wood, stone, ores, limestone, salt, pottery and heavy goods which were conveyed along its narrow streets. The village boasts two lifeboat houses, visible in both these images. The two houses are indicated above, with (1) showing the house of 1869, which was used until 1927, and was sited high up on the hill on the east side of the village, and (2) the later boathouse of 1927 to 1933. This boathouse is now used for the inshore lifeboat. (By courtesy of Matt Main)

MARKET PLACE, PORT ISAAC

Gavern, with the boats' cargoes being offloaded onto the beach and any that fell to the sand considered common property.

The main employment for the populations of Port Isaac and Port Gaverne, however, came from the huge shoals of pilchards which annually visited the bay. The cellars where the pilchards were cured are still intact and used by the fishermen of Port Isaac today. Previously this building offered safe storage for the village pilot rowing gigs, as it does today. At Port Gaverne the remains of a lime kiln can be seen, as well as three cellars, two of which have recently been converted into holiday accommodation.

By the early twentieth century pilchards ceased to appear in the bay and the winter herring fishery became of paramount importance. Herring were salted like pilchards, and smoked as kippers. The fishing boats were laid up in the summer and the men would go off crewing the yachts of the inter-war period, such as the great 'J' class vessels out of Cowes. These old mariners could at one time be seen strolling on the Platt or standing outside the old lifeboat station sharing a yarn with their blue seaman jumpers proudly carrying the names of the great yachts of their past.

In the mid-1940s the herring shoals also disappeared and smaller yachts and dinghies replaced the larger yachts. With the building of railway and better roads linking Cornwall more and more visitors came to the county, and they soon found that the village offered much in the way of holiday attractions. Mains water, electricity and modern sanitation, with the introduction of a proper sewage plant,

This fine historic photograph taken at the turn of the century looks up the 'narrows' from what is today the lifeboat station. The building facing the camera, with the sign board mounted on the wall, is the premises of the Sherratt family, the village bakers at the time. This fine building is now the popular Mote Restaurant. A dozen or so local gentlemen are gathered among the hauled up fishing boats on the Platt, no doubt swapping a yarn or two, and some of whom would be members of the lifeboat crew. The white-bearded gentleman with the child to the left is the great grandfather of Deputy Launching Authority and former Helmsman Nigel Sherratt, who continues his family's long association with the village and its lifeboat operations. (By courtesy of Nigel Sherratt)

An aerial view of the harbour showing the lifeboat station situated at the head of the slipway with the triangular structure to the right forming the historic fish cellars dating back to the sixteenth century and now owned by Port Isaac Fishermen Ltd, home to the ILB from 1967 to 1994. Today, in addition to providing workshops and storage for the local fishermen's tackle and equipment, a fish trading business is carried on from within the building, which is also used as a storage facility for two of Port Isaac Rowing Club's pilot gigs.

accelerated Port Isaac's change from a fishing village to a holiday resort, with the quaint fisherman's cottages becoming primarily holiday accommodation as the inhabitants moved to new houses at the top of the hill. Tourism plays an increasingly important role and dominates the village's economy.

Today, the village has gained international recognition as the TV village of Port Wen, home to the long-running TV series 'Doc Martin' starring Martin Clunes, which has led to visitors from around the world coming to see where the TV doctor does his work. However, the village retains its historic charm, and most of the old centre of the village consists of eighteenth and nineteenth century cottages, many of which are officially listed as of architectural or historic importance, lining narrow alleys and 'opes' winding down steep hillsides. Meanwhile, in the late twentieth century the fishermen began to concentrate on shellfish and mackerel during the summer months, and today crab and lobster form the main catches as fishing and fish-processing continues to offer a degree of work in the village. Currently there are five full-time fishing boats and one part-timer operating from the port, but in the 1950s there was an active mackerel fleet in addition to a dozen or more boats moored in the harbour.

The First Lifeboat

The lifeboat station at Port Isaac was established in 1869 and was one of many established in Cornwall and the West Country by the Royal National Lifeboat Institution (RNLI) during the second half of the nineteenth century as the organisation looked to expand operations. Lifeboats had already been supplied to Bude (1853), Padstow (1856) and Newquay (1860), and the lifeboat station at Port Isaac was established mainly to provide better protection for the fishing boats which used the area, and operated from adjacent coves, which often had to run to harbour at considerable risk in bad weather.

The coast around Port Isaac is very dangerous, with steep cliffs and few landing beaches. Abnormal ground seas, which often arise without warning, are common in the area and shipwrecks were frequent in the days of sail, when the vessels would be driven ashore, helpless in the face of a westerly gale. Ten years before the establishment of the station, Charles Mitchell, a local fisherman,

The first Port Isaac lifeboat, Richard and Sarah, was on station from 1869 to 1887. She is pictured being recovered up Fore Street, approaching the Golden Lion, with crew and helpers at the ropes. The shore helper in the foreground, carrying a carriage shifting bar over his shoulder, was known as a 'stick man'. Behind the lifeboat, a supporting beam can be seen between the buildings.

gained distinction by leading three trips, at great risk to himself, to rescue four men from the sloop *Busy*, of Newquay, which was wrecked nearby on 25 October 1859. In recognition of his brave efforts, the RNLI had awarded him the Silver medal for gallantry.

The opening of the station at Port Isaac followed a visit to the area, in June 1869, of the RNLI's Inspector. He stated that: 'a lifeboat would be useful and especially to the crews of fishing boats which sometimes had to run for the Port at great risk.' He recommended a standard 32ft self-righter be supplied, but while there were sufficient boatmen to form a crew, the local committee would only be able to contribute a few pounds annually towards the running costs. Port Isaac was, in the nineteenth century, a small and relatively poor fishing village, and raising funds for the cause would have strained the resources of many locals. In the event, the station's operation was overseen largely by the Honorary Secretary and attempts to establish a local committee were unsuccessful.

The sum of £700 given to the RNLI by Mr and Mrs Richard Thornton West, of Streatham and Exeter, was appropriated to pay for the station. Named *Richard and Sarah*, the first lifeboat measured 32ft by 7ft 7in, pulled ten oars, and had a crew of thirteen, made up by local boatmen. She was built by Messrs Forrestt, of Limehouse, the RNLI's preferred boatbuilder of the era. She was ready by late September 1869, and was brought to Cornwall by rail, with the Bristol and Exeter Railway company transporting her free of charge from Bristol to Exeter, and then the Cornwall Railway

The first Richard and Sarah on her carriage in the street. She had a light blue hull and was distinguishable by the elliptical plate mounted on her bow which carried the words 'National Lifeboat Institution'. In the early days the lifeboat crew were called by bugle. On occasions the coxswain would throw nuts into the air and the men would rush to pick them up. The nuts became available in the area from time to time after a visit from the schooners running to Spain.

Company took it on free from Exeter to Bodmin. An account of the boat's arrival, published in the *Western Daily Mercury*, shows how much the inhabitants of the district appreciated the opening of this station, which was a significant event:

'The lifeboat arrived with gear at Bodmin Road Station on 5 October 1869. Here it was met by a team of eight horses kindly lent by the merchants of Wadebridge. At Bodmin it remained for an hour for the inspection of the inhabitants; from here it proceeded to Wadebridge for the night. Early next morning it left via St Minver and St Endellion with eight horses lent by farmers of St Endellion. At Trewetha, about a mile from Port Isaac, they were met to form a procession by Capt Ward (Lifeboat Inspector), the local Committee, the Rev Smith, Vicar of St Minver, a band, then the boat on her carriage bearing two flags. She contained the crew dressed in white frocks and red caps, holding aloft their oars, while the horses were decorated with ribbons. On arrival at the beach Captain Ward gave an excellent speech to 2,000 to 3,000 people. After launching, rowing and sailing exercises, the boat was fastened to a vessel by means of tackle. She was then turned over with her crew, righting in less than a minute, and freeing of water in a few seconds.'

The boat was christened by Miss Trevan, daughter of the Chairman of the local Committee, who also placed a bottle containing coins and documents below the foundation stone of the boathouse. This house stood on a site presented by Lord Robartes, who made other generous gifts to the Institution at this period, including new lifeboats for Porthleven and Fowey. At the time of the naming ceremony, work on the boathouse had only just started, and so the lifeboat was initially kept in a fish store until the new building was ready.

As a site for the boathouse among the few houses at the bottom of the valley could not be found, it had to be built up the hill on the eastern side, out towards the mouth of the harbour, on a level piece of ground in the area where the school was to be built. The road running down to the beach was very steep and narrow, and, in order to launch the boat, it had to be taken several hundred yards through streets which, in places, were extremely narrow and afforded less than a foot clearance to the carriage. At one corner, there were only two inches between its sides and the houses, and so getting the boat afloat was a challenging and often time-consuming procedure.

In 1870 and 1871 work was undertaken to slightly widen the passage, and a low wall was built at the top of the cliff in front of the boathouse prevent people, who were helping to haul the lifeboat in or out of the house, falling over the edge. And in May 1871 the Inspector reported that, 'The narrow street ... had been much improved and there was now no difficulty in getting her down'. When the boat was descending, a few people went ahead to steer the carriage, while the other helpers held on to the ropes behind in order to prevent boat and carriage running away. The rather remarkable, and in many ways spectacular launching arrangements became well known and subsequently many photographs were published and even films made of the launch. One of the best known lifeboat photographs in existence is that of the Port Isaac boat negotiating a sharp corner on her carriage.

The first service of the first lifeboat took place on 24 October 1870, when the Genoese brig *Stephano Grosso* was driven against the cliffs and began to break up rapidly in a heavy north-westerly gale. The rocket apparatus, which was first brought to the scene, managed to save all but three of the crew, but then the lines broke and could not be repaired. The lifeboat was immediately launched and proceeded to the wreck where, with much difficulty, her crew succeeded in saving those who were still on board. Charles Mitchell, who had been awarded a Silver medal eleven years previously, showed great courage again, firstly while in charge of the rocket apparatus, and later in the lifeboat. As a result, the RNLI voted him a Silver Bar to his medal.

The lifeboat house built in 1869-70 at a cost of £230 on the hill leading out of the village to the east. The iron railings in front of the boathouse were provided in 1893 to prevent school children from cutting and defacing the doors. The house had not been completed when the Boat arrived on 6 October 1869, so she was stored in the Good Intent Cellar, which was demolished in 1877 to make way for the school.

Two years later, on 20 November 1872, the lifeboat put off at daybreak to two local fishing luggers, *Castle* and *J.T.K.*, which were at anchor in a dangerous position, in a heavy ground swell with no wind, and saved the two boats with their crews of four.

For her next life-saving service, which took place on 20 February 1877, *Richard and Sarah* was taken four miles on her carriage over some of the steepest and narrowest roads in the county to Port Quin, where she was launched to help the barque *Ada Melmore*. This vessel, of Maryport, bound from Glasgow for Montevideo, had anchored close to some rocks in a heavy north-westerly gale, and was flying a signal of distress. After a difficult launch, the lifeboat reached the casualty, but the master and officers refused to leave. The crew, however, decided otherwise, and ten were brought ashore by the lifeboat. Later, when the weather had moderated, the men were put back again, and the barque eventually weighed anchor and succeeded in getting under way.

On 25 March 1880 the lifeboat capsized twice while on exercise in what was a rather unusual incident which, fortunately, did not result in any loss of life, as all twelve crew on board regained the boat. The RNLI District Inspector visited the station on 31 March to ascertain why the boat capsized and held an inquiry in the presence of the Chairman and Honorary Secretary. Surprisingly, the lifeboat had been launched on exercise with the intention of the Coxswain to see whether she could be capsized. She was first

turned over when on the starboard tack, with smooth water and the wind blowing a moderate gale offshore. The boat was sailed with her lee gunwale six to twelve inches under water and a considerable amount of water was taken on board, while the crew were sitting to windward and the sheets were occasionally eased.

When a squall suddenly struck, although the sheets and halyards were let go, it was too late and the boat capsized. The crew were thrown out to leeward except two who were taken all the way round in her. When she went over, the keel remained about two feet from the water, her masts and sails were nearly horizontal and remained so for about three minutes, and the buoyancy was insufficient to lift the sails out of the water. When these were unhooked, the boat was righted with the crew having to weigh down on her keel and bilge wale. As soon as the masts and sails came out of the water, the boat came round, and the eight men were able to climb back on board. However, she was so full of water that she went completely round again, tipping the men back into the water. This time, as they had been unhooked, the sails did not stop her and she came to rest in an upright position. At this point, the Coxswain ordered that the boat be given time to empty herself, which she did quickly, and the crew got safely on board again and returned ashore. The whole incident lasted only about ten minutes.

During his visit, the Inspector took the lifeboat afloat in a fresh breeze and found her sails – a dipping lug and mizzen – to be the right size, and not too large as the crew claimed. The crew who had been involved in the capsize were again in the boat and they had not lost confidence in her, but rather the opposite. In righting herself, the boat had shown the crew 'her good qualities', and the Coxswain, Frederick Trevan, was blamed for 'carrying on beyond all reason', according to the Inspector's report. The Inspector drew his attention 'to the danger of sailing lifeboats when half full of water and with the gunwale buried'. The boat had not been damaged by the incident, and none of her gear had been lost.

On his visit, the Inspector also found the station to be 'in good order', but noted that 'the subscriptions were necessarily small, there was no working committee, [and so] the affairs of the Branch were being managed by the Honorary Secretary assisted by a gentleman. Things were a little out of order owing to the recent capsize, ropes being out to dry, but all were speedily replaced and the boat satisfactorily launched and exercised. The accident had in no way interfered with the readiness of the men.' So despite the capsize, and the somewhat rash actions of the Coxswain, the station continued to be in a good operational state.

The lifeboat effected a very timely launch on 26 March 1882, when, at about 1pm, the schooner *British Queen*, bound from her home port of Wexford for Porthcawl in ballast, was seen in distress in a strong north-westerly gale and heavy seas. The crew, four in number, were seen leaving the ship in their own boat about a mile offshore. Fortunately, the lifeboat reached them when they were about 100 yards from a cliff under which any rescue would have proved almost impossible. During the launching of the lifeboat, one of the shore helpers, Robert Broad, had an accident when letting go of the lashings of the carriage, and lost a little finger with his arm also being injured. He was subsequently voted £10 in compensation, and in September 1882 a further £20 as his injuries were quite severe. The RNLI also paid his medical expenses of £29 2s 2d.

On the morning of 7 February 1883 several fishing boats put to sea from Port Isaac in fine weather and a completely smooth sea. Shortly before noon, however, a ground sea suddenly rose up, placing the boats in danger as they were unable to enter the harbour. *Richard and Sarah* was soon launched and she managed to tow in four of them, with seven men, and then stood by as the others came in.

An occasion on which many lives might have been lost was the foundering of the steamship *Indus*, of Dundee, off Trevose, while she was bound from Cardiff to Tenerife with a cargo of coal on 14 October 1886. The lifeboat was launched and found two of her boats, containing the crew of twenty-nine and a stowaway, drifting along the coast trying to find a place to land. She took on board twenty-five of these, while a fishing vessel which was nearby brought back the remaining five, with the boats and their crews facing a strong north-westerly breeze and heavy seas during this service. The lifeboat was back at Port Isaac by 8.20am, fifty minutes after the casualty had first been sighted two miles out at sea.

Although this proved to be the last rescue performed by the first *Richard and Sarah* lifeboat, with a new boat of the same name replacing her in October 1887, another incident three days later, on 17 October 1886, saw her crew's and the station's efficiency being questioned. The barque *Sarah Anderson*, of Liverpool, was lost off Tintagel Head the lifeboat was requested but was unable to launch due to the prevailing conditions. One of the witnesses to the wreck, a Mr Bastard , who was described as a retired master mariner, stated that a double hauling off warp and anchor warp should be supplied for Port Isaac lifeboat.

The actions of those in charge of the lifeboat was also examined by the Committee ,and it was admitted by all that it was impossible to have launched the lifeboat. The conclusion was reached that nothing more could have been done and that the conduct of the Coastguard as well as the lifeboat men should be commended.

The RNLI's Committee later informed the Board of Trade that the station already had a single warp and that a double one, as suggested by Mr Bastard, would be of no benefit.

There was an unusual way of selecting villagers to help launch the lifeboat on exercises at the turn of the century. According to Geoff Provis, author of *The Seafarers of Port Isaac*, volunteers needed to launch the boat would be paid a small sum, and such was the poverty in the village that a system of choosing helpers was devised as there always more shore crew than were needed. In order to select who should help, the coxswain threw metal badges marked RNLI into the crowd, shouting 'scramblers' as he tossed them in the air. The first men to pick up a badge would then assist with the launch and recovery of the lifeboat. It was said that the younger men pulled back the older men, who often walked away with tears in their eyes. Those that picked up a badge would go to Mrs Sherratt's bakery and she would give them some food, paid for by the RNLI.

A fine photograph of the first Richard and Sarah, which was on station from 1869 to 1887, as she slides off her carriage into the calm waters of the harbour. The gentleman in the centre on the beach, dressed in plus fours, appears to be a photographer taking his opportunity to record the event, which is enjoyed by plenty of other onlookers. (By courtesy of Port Isaac RNLI)

A second Richard and Sarah Lifeboat

I n June 1887 the self-righting ability of the 1869-built *Richard and Sarah* lifeboat was questioned and, as she was almost twenty years old, a replacement was deemed necessary so a new lifeboat, 'possessing all the latest improvements as early as possible', was ordered. The new boat was a self-righter, like her predecessor, but two feet longer, measuring 34ft by 7ft 6in, and rowing the same number of oars. She was fitted with two water ballast tanks, and had been built by Forrestt & Son, of Limehouse, in London, the RNLI's preferred boatbuilders of the late nineteenth century. The new lifeboat passed her harbour trial on 4 October 1887, and preparations were then made to get her to her station.

A great turn-out of people watch the launch of the second Richard and Sarah as the crew take their first haul on the oars, pulling the lifeboat off the launching carriage, before heading out to sea. The quickest launch from the original boathouse was about four minutes. (By courtesy of RNLI Port Isaac)

On 24 October 1887 she was brought from London by the Great Western Railway to St Columb railway station, while the District Inspector went to Padstow to make arrangements for the transfer of the new boat. He sent the Padstow carriage to Truro which was used to bring the boat back to Padstow, where she arrived on 28 October. The crew from Port Isaac then went to Padstow in order to take the new boat back, accompanied by the

The third Richard and Sarah is hauled up to the 'narrows' with mixture of crew and helpers lending a hand to the heaving cables through the 'narrows'. (By courtesy of RNLI Port Isaac)

District Inspector. He found on reaching Port Isaac that several alterations were necessary to the carriage, pending which the boat was hauled up on skids at Porth Gaverne, about half a mile away, whence she could be easily launched. With the arrival of a new self-righter, the old boat was sold locally.

Among the changes to the station personnel during the first few years of the new boat being on station was the resignation in December 1887 of Pascoe Brown, who had been Second Coxswain for eighteen years and had to leave the crew due to old age. During his time, the boat had launched eight times on service and saved fifty-seven lives, and the committee voted him £5. Two years later, the Honorary Secretary Mr Trevan passed away; he had held the post for about three years, and was succeeded by William Guy, who had been Secretary in the early 1880s.

The new lifeboat was named *Richard and Sarah*, like her predecessor, having been funded by Mr & Mrs Thornton West, Streatham. The second *Richard and Sarah* performed several notable services, the first being a most arduous one which was carried out in a very strong north-westerly gale. On 7 November 1890 the Penzance schooner *Golden Light*, bound from Newport for Hayle, with coal, was sighted in rough sea about four miles off Port Isaac, apparently making for Port Quin bay. A messenger later arrived from Port Quin saying she had anchored and had lost her mainmast. The lifeboat was taken by carriage, pulled by a team of fourteen horses, to Port Quin cove, where she arrived about noon, and was readied for launching. Because of the prevailing conditions, this had to be delayed until 10pm, but she safely got afloat and the crew, after two hours of hard pulling, reached the disabled schooner. Five of the schooner's crew had already been brought ashore at Port Quin by a fishing boat, the remaining five being rescued with difficulty by the lifeboat, as the vessel was rolling heavily. These were landed at Port Isaac at 2.30am on 8 November.

A very gallant rescue was carried out by the lifeboat on 2 January 1895, with great demands made upon the stamina and endurance of her crew. A collier, bound from Newport to Santos, had suffered a terrible battering in a gale in the Channel, and was drifting shoreward with bowsprit, fore and main topmasts and all working gear carried away, and totally helpless. When first sighted, the vessel, the barque *Antoinette*, of St John's, New Brunswick, was about eight miles off. To reach her, the lifeboat crew had a hard pull to get clear of the land, and then set sail, but just before she reached the scene a steam tug took the vessel in tow, and made for Padstow.

Richard and Sarah caught up with the tug and barque, and remained in attendance during the passage to safety. All went well until *Antoinette* was entering the harbour, where, as the tide was low and the vessel not under proper control, she struck the notorious Doom Bar. The tow rope broke, leaving her aground and broadside to the sea. Just off the port, the Padstow lifeboat *Arab* had arrived on scene, and, together with the Port Isaac boat, she was taken alongside the stranded ship, which was lying in the heaviest breakers. *Richard and Sarah* rescued ten of the barque's crew, and *Arab* four, all of whom were landed at Padstow by 3pm. The Port Isaac boat immediately returned to her station, battling heavy weather on the return and arriving at 7.30pm. The crew had been on service for about eleven hours, and were thoroughly wet and exhausted after their trying experience.

In December 1895 James Haynes retired from his position as Coxswain, having been in the post since the station was established in 1869. During his twenty-six years as Coxswain, he had been out on service eleven times and assisted to save seventy-two lives. In recognition of the fine service he had given to the station and the RNLI, he was presented with the Silver medal, a gratuity of £25 and a Certificate of Service.

On 1 October 1899 the small steamship *Lynx*, of Cardiff, left Portreath for Port Talbot, but when off Hartland experienced engine trouble. In the strong north-easterly wind, and with her engines running intermittently, she tried to make Padstow, but a change in the wind prevented her from getting there and she was forced to anchor and signal for assistance. *Richard and Sarah* was launched at 3pm and took off her crew of seven as a precautionary measure, while the vessel was left to ride out the storm. The lifeboat was accordingly left on the beach to take the crew back if possible, but during the night *Lynx* parted her cable and drove on the rocks, where she became a total wreck.

The lifeboat completed her next service during the evening of 24 November 1902, this time to help some fishing boats. They had been unable to get back ashore in a south-westerly gale, very

All hands to haul: the second Richard and Sarah being pulled up through the 'narrows', inch by inch. The Coxswain is keeping a close eye on the carriage wheel so as to avoid the rig becoming jammed between the buildings. The carriage and lifeboat weight approximately six and half tons in total. (By courtesy of RNLI Port Isaac)

Taking the strain: the second Richard and Sarah being pulled back to the boathouse watched by, among others, a group of children standing on top of the harbour wall. The recovery of the lifeboat was an exhausting operation, and at least forty strong hands were usually needed at the heaving ropes. (By courtesy of RNLI Port Isaac)

Opposite: One of the many fine photos showing the Port Isaac lifeboat being hauled through the streets back to the lifeboat station. This one depicts the second Richard and Sarah with a crowd of helpers getting ready to haul on the ropes and pull boat and carriage up the hill back to the lifeboat station.

Below: The lifeboat being taken through the challenging right hand turning point past the Golden Lion Inn to enter the Narrows; this was the most difficult manoeuvre when launching, with a crew member walking ahead with a sturdy iron-shod wooden bar over his shoulder ready to apply this to the forward carriage wheels if necessary; a mistake could result in the lifeboat becoming wedged between the buildings.

heavy ground sea and low tide, and, although the wind later veered to north-westerly, it did not abate. *Richard and Sarah* put off soon after 10pm and stood by while the tide turned, and at high water towed in four of the boats, one by one, and helped another two to safe moorings.

On 11 September 1903 the Port Isaac crew carried out a fine service when *Richard and Sarah* saved a vessel abandoned as a total loss by her crew. During a north-westerly gale with heavy ground sea the French brig *Union*, of Auray, bound for Port Talbot with a cargo of pit-wood, became waterlogged off Port Isaac, and hoisted a signal of distress. The lifeboat was launched and stood by the anchored vessel for some time, but the weather did not improve and it was thought advisable to land the crew and all six men were brought ashore. On 13 September, however, the brig was still riding at her anchors, and as the weather had moderated the captain said he wanted to try to save her. So the lifeboat took the crew back, and some lifeboatmen went on board to help pump and weigh anchor. The vessel, kept afloat by her cargo, was successfully brought into Padstow. In recognition of their fine efforts, the crew were each granted additional awards of five shillings.

During the late 1890s and into the early years of the twentieth century the station's location, and in fact its existence, was questioned. In July 1897 the RNLI considered moving the

353 A Tight Fit with the Lifeboat at Port Isaac

boathouse as the position of the existing one was deemed rather dangerous, and taking the boat through the narrow streets, which were often crowded with children, was a hazardous operation. A better site for a new boathouse was available on Fore Street at the Platt, close to the beach, at a rent of about £14 a year. A larger boat with a drop keel was also wanted by Coxswain and crew as they often had to cover significant distances to reach casualties, and a drop keel would enable them to sail rather than row to a casualty. However, the Chief Inspector recommended that a decision about the station's future be postponed until the steam lifeboat had arrived at Padstow and been assessed, as he doubted whether a lifeboat at Port Isaac would then be needed, apart from some beach work and keeping an eye on the fishing boats.

In October 1901 the situation was again assessed, by when Padstow's steam lifeboat had come and, rather tragically, gone. Built in 1899 and named *James Stevens No.4*, the 56ft 6in steam lifeboat had been on station for only just over a year when she was wrecked on service. On 11 April 1900, with a stormy north-westerly wind blowing, the ketch *Peace and Plenty* went ashore. The Padstow pulling lifeboat Arab went out to help but, while at anchor close to the casualty, was struck by a tremendous sea that broke ten oars and washed eight of her crew overboard. The men managed to regain the lifeboat without loss, but the boat was wrecked on the rocks and became a total loss. The steam lifeboat was launched but was caught by a heavy swell as she was leaving harbour and capsized,

The second Richard and Sarah about to be launched. In December 1892 a new launching carriage was supplied to the station; it was built by Bristol Wagon Works Co and was forwarded to the station from Bristol per Great Western Railway to Wadebridge, and then by road. (By courtesy of Port Isaac RNLI)

with eight of her crew of eleven being drowned. She later came ashore, a complete wreck, and was subsequently broken up.

In place of the steam lifeboat, a unique arrangement was devised whereby a steam tug, purpose-built by the RNLI for life-saving work and named *Helen Peele*, was used to pull a large sailing lifeboat, the 42ft self-righter *Edmund Harvey*, to the scene of a casualty. This arrangement worked very well for almost thirty years, and its effectiveness had a significant bearing on the situation at Port Isaac, where demand for the lifeboat dropped. In view of these developments, the District inspector reported that he could not recommend expenditure on a new boathouse in a better position at Port Isaac and deemed the present arrangement, with the lifeboat being taken through the streets, adequate. But he did not recommend closure of the station, as the local fishing fleet was active and thriving, and so a lifeboat was needed. However, a larger boat could not be used due to the launching restrictions, the present 34ft lifeboat would be replaced by the first available sound lifeboat of the same dimensions.

In October 1904 an assessment was made by the RNLI's Chief Inspector of the best site for the station. During his regular visit, he had the boat launched at low-water at Port Gaverne, three quarters

The launch and recovery of the lifeboat made great demands on the village's small male population, but they were often assisted by visitors and sometimes the women. Careful control of the lifeboat on her carriage, weighing more than five tons, was needed in order to manoeuvre the rig down the steep incline of Fore Street, negotiate the Narrows and on down to the harbour slip, and the same effort was needed to haul the boat back to the station. The photo above right shows what is probably a visitor in his Sunday best taking the strain on a downward run. The other photo has the men at full stretch during the recovery of the boat.

of a mile east of Port Isaac, and then proceeded to Port Quin, four miles west of Port Isaac, both of which places were being assessed as alternative launching sites. The boat was finally recovered at Port Isaac. Port Gaverne was assessed as a launch site, but the conclusion was that to pull the lifeboat out from there in at north-westerly gale was 'a physical impossibility', but in the same conditions the boat could be got out of Port Isaac. The Chief Inspector also carefully examined Port Quin as a place for launching when adverse weather prevented a launch from Port Isaac. While it was possible to pull the boat out, the channel was so narrow that it would be dangerous to return.

The Chief Inspector held a meeting with the Honorary Secretary, station officer of the Coast Guard, two Coxswains, the bowmen and two representatives from the crew to decide on what was needed for the station. It was unanimously agreed that a larger boat than the present one could not be launched, while moving the boathouse from its present position was not necessary, but that a boat with a drop keel was necessary. The Inspector stated that *Reserve No.7* lifeboat would be supplied, initially on temporary duty as an experiment, and the station lifeboat be brought to London the name of the present boat being transferred to the reserve boat. And finally, that once every two years the lifeboat would be launched on exercise at Port Quin Bay, and be recovered at Port Gaverne from where she would be brought by road to her house. Following these discussions, and the provision of another boat, the station's operation remained unaltered for the next decade, until the outbreak of war.

However, before the new lifeboat had arrived, the second *Richard and Sarah* and her crew were involved in a tragedy which struck the Port Isaac fishing fleet on 9 December 1904. At about 7pm, as the fishing boats were returning to harbour heavily laden with their catches, a heavy ground sea overwhelmed one boat and sank her as she made for Port Gaverne. As several boats were still out and the ground sea had increased, *Richard and Sarah* was launched and helped three of them in. The crew of the swamped boat were drowned, but it happened so quickly that the lifeboat could not, under any circumstances, have reached the scene in time to effect a rescue.

However, details of the loss soon became known in the village, and a crowd attempted to storm the boathouse with some blaming the lifeboat crew for not launching sooner. Only with some difficulty was the Honorary Secretary able to restore order, and then get the lifeboat launched to help the other boats. In assessing the events subsequently, the RNLI's Deputy Chief Inspector recommended that when the fishing fleet was out and their return might prove difficult and dangerous, it would make sense to have the lifeboat taken down to the beach in case she was needed, and the Honorary Secretary agreed.

This proved to be the last service carried out by the second *Richard and Sarah* lifeboat, as the RNLI had decided to send another lifeboat to the station when it became available, and by early 1905 a suitable boat was ready. So, in January 1905, upon the arrival of the new boat, the second *Richard and Sarah* lifeboat was returned to the RNLI's London Storeyard via the London and South Western Railway Company. During her eighteen years at Port Isaac she had launched nine times on service and saved twenty-eight lives.

The last pulling lifeboats

ollowing the decision by the RNLI's Committee of Management in 1904 to supply another lifeboat, an 1892-built 34ft self-righter was allocated to Port Isaac. Named *Charles Whitton* when built but redesignated Reserve No.7 in 1899, she was sent from London on 10 January 1905, via the London and South Western Railway to the Port Isaac Road railway station. She was renamed *Richard and Sarah*, becoming the third lifeboat to be so named. She had previously served the Drogheda No.1 station on Ireland's east coast, and was sent to Port Isaac on a trial basis, although ended up staying for more than two decades. Although the same size as her predecessor, the third *Richard and Sarah* was deemed to be a better boat and in better condition. However, her service calls were few and far between, and most of the casualties in the area were dealt with by the Padstow lifeboats.

In September 1905 the District Inspector reported on the biennial exercise of the boat from Port Quin Bay, and found great difficulties in launching from there, notably the time it took to get there and the cost. He stated that any boats in danger to the east

The 34ft self-righter Richard and Sarah, the last of that name, was on station from 1905 to 1927 having previously been at Drogheda No.1 station from 1892 to 1905, where she was named Charles Whitton. On board the lifeboat is Joseph Honey, who was Coxswain from 1910 to 1920. (By courtesy of the RNLI)

The third Richard and Sarah being got ready for launching, with the 'stick men' in the foreground followed by station officials. (By courtesy of Port Isaac RNLI)

of Pentire Head could be more effectively helped by the Padstow steam tug and sailing lifeboat. The crew were also somewhat against going to Port Quin for launching and considered it unnecessary as they could reach the area more quickly by sea.

A number of personnel changes took place shortly after the third *Richard and Sarah* was on station. In October 1908 John Haynes, who had been Coxswain for seven years, resigned due to ill health aged fifty-seven and was granted a pension and presented with a Certificate of Service. His replacement, Thomas Mitchell Collins, remained in post less than two years, retiring in July 1910 as he was away so much from home that he was unable to fulfil his duties effectively. And in October 1911 long-serving Honorary Secretary Dr R. Julyan George resigned because he was leaving the locality. He had been in the post for more than eighteen years and he was accorded the Thanks of the Institution on Vellum in recognition of his services.

The first service call at Port Isaac by the third *Richard and Sarah* came shortly before noon on 7 December 1911, when the coastguard reported that a schooner, anchored a mile offshore, had parted one of her cables and was being driven towards the land. The lifeboat crew launched but, on reaching the vessel, the schooner *Berthe Marie*, of Brest, it was found that her cable was holding. As there appeared to be a strong possibility of it breaking, however, with disastrous results, the lifeboat took off the crew of four and brought them ashore, apart from the master, who refused to leave. Fortunately the vessel's anchors held, and the next day the lifeboat took the crew back and put them on board. The sailors, however, were unable to raise the *Berthe Marie's* anchors, so the

The third Richard and Sarah between the buildings surrounding the harbour Platt, beginning the journey up the hill to the boathouse. Note the heavy wooden prop adding strength to the walls of the old buildings either side. (By courtesy of RNLI Port Isaac)

The launch of the lifeboat created as much excitement then, as can be seen from this evocative photograph from the 1920s, as it does today. A crowd of enthusiastic visitors and locals follow behind the third Richard and Sarah as she reaches the harbour. (By courtesy of RNLI Port Isaac)

The third Richard and Sarah is manoeuvred through the streets; this photograph shows just what a tight fit it was for the carriage and lifeboat with, in places, just two inches to spare. (By courtesy of RNLI Port Isaac)

The third Richard and Sarah being drawn up through the streets, just about reaching the sharp turning left outside what is today Fearless Store; note the cables that have set into grooves – which can still be seen – within the sides of the buildings. Ropes and pulleys had to be used to ease the boat down the hill and around the sharp bend at the bottom of Fore Street. The whole operation, which was often photographed, often saw everyone in the village turning out to assist, or at least watch the spectacle. (By courtesy of RNLI Port Isaac)

lifeboatmen went on board and helped to raise them. As the wind was then favourable, the schooner went on her way up Channel. However, four days later the Mumbles lifeboat had to be launched to assist in saving her. During this service, P.J. Mitchell was injured and subsequently received £4 as compensation.

The last two services performed by the third *Richard and Sarah* were both, by coincidence, to the same local fishing vessel, *Flossie*. On 30 May 1913, this boat, with one person on board, was seen to be shipping much water while making for home in a southerly gale, putting her in considerable danger. The lifeboat found *Flossie* two miles north of Port Isaac, and stood by her until she reached safety. On the morning of 14 October 1915, *Flossie* again became weather bound a short distance along the coast. The occupant, an old man, pulled for two hours towards the shore in a heavy ground sea, and when near the coastguard station signalled for help. The lifeboat put off and took him on board, while two of the lifeboat crew brought in his boat.

During 1917–18 it became necessary to close the station temporarily owing to shortage of man power, as most of the village's able-bodied male inhabitants had enrolled in the Royal and Merchant Navies. In September 1916 sufficient men had been available should the lifeboat be required, but by March 1917 the RNLI's Inspector reported that the boat had not been afloat since August 1916 and a crew could not be found for an exercise; most

About forty men heave the third Richard and Sarah down to the water for a launch, during the early years of the twentieth century before the breakwaters were constructed to provide the cover with some shelter. (By courtesy of RNLI Port Isaac)

A special day with the band playing and many spectators greeting the third Richard and Sarah; note the 'stick' man clearly visible in the foreground. In October 1904 the RNLI's Committee of Management decided, in light of a recommendation made by the District Inspector, the two men employed in the shaft of the carriage be paid one shilling each extra, both for exercise and service launches, because of 'the difficult nature of the work and with a view of always getting the same man'. (By courtesy of RNLI Port Isaac)

of those available were aged sixty to seventy years, and so closing the station temporarily was the only option.

On 12 April 1918 the lifeboat was launched on service manned by a scratch crew; both Coxswains were away and only six men who had been on the boat before were left. During this period, however, a subsidised auxiliary motor fishing boat, *Willing Boys*, acted as a rescue boat, and performed one successful service. This took place on 15 May 1918, when she landed fifteen persons from the steamship *Mars*, of Bergen, which stranded at Port Quin Bay in dense fog. In September 1919, when the villagers had returned from war service, the RNLI decided that the station should be reopened as a full crew was available.

During the 1920s considerable alterations were made at Port Isaac in the arrangements for launching the lifeboat. The Institution acquired some old cottages at the bottom of the village, across the road from the beach, and built a new boathouse on their site,

A high water launch of the third Richard and Sarah. (By courtesy of RNLI Port Isaac)

Following the launch, Richard and Sarah is pulled away from the beach by the ten oarsmen that make up her crew. (By courtesy of RNLI Port Isaac)

Recovering the third Richard and Sarah was a labour-intensive process, particularly at low water. The launchers haul on the ropes to get the boat off the beach and up the slipway. (By courtesy of RNLI Port Isaac)

The third Richard and Sarah outside the lifeboat house on the east side of the village. In November 1911 a lowering post was fixed at the rear of boathouse at a cost of £2 4s, and in May 1912 a lowering bollard was provided, both measures to help improve launching arrangements. (By courtesy of Port Isaac RNLI)

which was completed in 1927. Two breakwaters, running out from the cliff on each side of the harbour, were built between 1926 and 1932, with the delay caused by the builder going out of business. It became possible to get the boat afloat much more rapidly than before, as the necessity for manoeuvring the carriage through the narrow streets – spectacular though it was as a sight for onlookers – was eliminated. However, an ex-coxswain of the Padstow lifeboats has been heard to say that it was a quicker launch from the old boathouse than the new one, owing to the latter being badly placed in relation to the slipway, but this was probably an exaggeration.

However, as it turned out, whether it was faster or not proved to be irrelevant as no service launches were performed after these

The third Richard and Sarah under sail and oar as she sets a course to the west of Port Isaac, up towards Tintagel. This is one of the few photographs showing the lifeboat under sail. For most of the pulling lifeboat era, the Coxswains and crews wanted a sailing lifeboat with a drop keel, which would have had a greater range, but such a boat would have been too large for launching through the streets. (By courtesy of RNLI Port Isaac)

The third Richard and Sarah, on station from 1905 to 1927, being hauled onto her carriage outside what is today the Nathan Outlaw Michelin-starred restaurant The Fish Kitchen. Despite the postcard being entitled 'A Lifeboat Launch', the boat is actually being recovered onto her carriage. (By courtesy of RNLI Port Isaac)

The third Richard and Sarah being readied for launching. (From an old postcard supplied by John Harrop)

Crowds watch as Richard and Sarah is launched. (By courtesy of Port Isaac RNLI)

alterations had been completed, and six years later the station was closed. By then the last of the Port Isaac pulling lifeboats, *Ernest Dresden*, built in 1917 for the Courtown station in County Wexford, had replaced *Richard and Sarah*, arriving in 1927 to take her place in the new boathouse. She was a self-righting craft measuring 35ft by 8ft 10in, rowed ten oars, and had already seen ten years of service prior to her arrival here. This lifeboat effected no rescues during her six years at Port Isaac and the station was closed in May 1933. The harbour had by then become badly silted, while the two motor lifeboats operating from the neighbouring Padstow station, in particular the large and powerful 61ft Barnett *Princess*

Mary, provided effective coverage of the area. Indeed, *Princess Mary* was used to tow *Ernest Dresden* away from the station in July 1933, with the boat going to the RNLI's Storeyard in Limehouse from where she was sold for £100 in December 1933. The two old boathouses were sold, with the later house of 1927 taken over by the Slipway House Hotel and used as a garage.

This fine view of the harbour, before the breakwaters were built in the 1920s, features the Old School House and the original lifeboat station situated on the eastern side of the village. Built in 1869 on land donated by Lord Robartes, the boathouse was used until 1927. (By courtesy of Port Isaac RNLI)

The third Richard and Sarah being beached after a launch. (By courtesy of Port Isaac RNLI)

The lifeboat house built in 1927 was used for the last six years of the station's pulling lifeboat operations. This photograph shows the building in the snow. (By courtesy of Port Isaac RNLI)

A view of the beach and cove from the east, where the original lifeboat house was built, showing the 1927 lifeboat house with a few small fishing boats pulled up on the beach. The 1927 building has been used by the inshore lifeboat since 1994. (By courtesy of Port Isaac RNLI)

With the oars set fair and the crew ready to pull, Ernest Dresden is readied to slip her carriage. Built in 1917 and stationed at Courtown until 1925, she was the last pulling lifeboat at Port Isaac. (By courtesy of RNLI Port Isaac)

Ernest Dresden being beached, with the crew poised to jump off and help the launchers with the recovery procedure. During the six years she spent at Port Isaac, Ernest Dresden never performed a service launch. She was sold out of service in December 1933. (By courtesy of RNLI Port Isaac)

Three photographs of Ernest Dresden being hauled up the beach to be recovered. (By courtesy of Port Isaac RNLI)

Throughout the history of Port Isaac lifeboat there has been support from the local community, and in this evocative photograph from the 1920s a young lady, named Inez Corey, is raising funds for the service using a homemade cardboard lifeboat collecting box with a display card around her neck. She was standing near the original lifeboat station in Fore Street, and is carrying the message 'Help the Lifeboat – Red Cross of the Sea'. Undoubtedly her dedicated efforts were much appreciated by the contemporary crew and committee.

When the station was closed, Ernest Dresden towed away in July 1933 by the Padstow lifeboat Princess Mary, a 61ft Barnett type built in 1929, and was subsequently taken to the RNLI's Storeyard at Limehouse, London, where she was stored until being sold in December 1933. (By courtesy of Port Isaac RNLI)

The first lifeboat house in the 1930s (left) after it had ceased being used for the lifeboat. The building was used as a post office during the 1980s (right), then a shop, and by 2015 had been converted into a gift shop with extensive alterations at the front. The boathouse is owned by Jon Cleave, whose family had long been associated with the RNLI and whose son, George Cleave, was on the ILB crew, while his great grandfather crewed the pulling and sailing lifeboats. (Left: Grahame Farr, by courtesy of the RNLI; right: Nicholas Leach)

An undated crew photograph, with the volunteers wearing their woolly hats and possibly the Coxswain holding the binoculars nearest camera. (By courtesy of RNLI Port Isaac)

The lifeboat crew pictured at the original lifeboat house in about 1925. The red wool hats identify the appointed crew members. Back row, left to right: Jack Hoskins, Jimmy Ros Can, Fred Honey, Captain Jack Provis, Walter Glover, Veth Brown; front row left to right, Jess Steer, Sam Bate, Tinker Brown, George Honey (Second Coxswain 1920-31 and Coxswain for the last two years of the station's operations), William H. Steer (Coxswain 1920-31) and Len Collings. (By courtesy of RNLI Port Isaac)

A fine body of men: Coxswain and crew standing outside the original lifeboat house, probably during the 1920s as they are wearing kapok life jackets, which were introduced in 1904. (By courtesy of RNLI Port Isaac)

The lifeboat crew in the early years of the twentieth century, wearing kapok lifejackets; unfortunately, the exact date of the photo and names of the crew are not known. Eleven crewmen are wearing red wool hats, while the Coxswain is wearing a peaked hat. The five men on the left were station officials, including the Honorary Secretary, who could be the man holding a telescope under his arm. The man second from the left has a side arms holster on his belt, possibly for carrying a flare gun. (By courtesy of RNLI Port Isaac)

The lifeboat house of 1927 was built on a site acquired by the RNLI following a demolition near the head of the beach. Although in a far more convenient position than the original boathouse, it was not ideally placed for the roadway down to the beach, and in the end was only used for six years as the station closed in 1933. It later became the garage for the Slipway House Hotel, as pictured in June 1970. (Grahame Farr, by courtesy of the RNLI)

The lifeboat house of 1927 pictured in August 1992, just before it was reacquired by the RNLI and converted for use by the D class inshore lifeboats. (Nicholas Leach)

Inshore Lifeboats

T he reopening of the lifeboat station at Port Isaac came about following the introduction of a new type of lifeboat in response to an increase in inshore incidents needing lifeboat assistance. In the 1950s and 1960s, as more people began using the sea for leisure, taking to yachts, dinghies and surfboards, so lifeboats were increasingly called out to help these leisure users. Conventional lifeboats, being slow and usually requiring at least seven crew, were not well suited to dealing with such incidents, many of which happened close to shore in relatively benign conditions. What was needed was a fast rescue craft which could respond speedily to incidents when a few minutes could make a crucial difference.

In 1962 the RNLI bought an inflatable boat for extensive trials, and a delegation visited France where similar boats were in operation, to see the boats in service. Following these initial steps, the first IRBs were introduced during the summer of 1963, when ten were sent to stations around England and Wales. Such

The first inshore lifeboat at Port Isaac was D-139, an RFD type inflatable measuring 15ft 6in by 6ft 4in and somewhat rudimentary compared to the RNLI's inshore lifeboats of the twenty-first century. (By courtesy of the RNLI)

Early rescue work and setting up the station

David Castle was heavily involved in the establishment of the station at Port Isaac in the mid-1960s, and then very much involved in its running thereafter, until his retirement in 1996 to Fuerteventura. He made his boat, Maid M (named after his children Martin, Andrew, Ian, David and Margaret), available for life-saving during the late 1950s and early 1960s (pictured below). She was built by Pearns of Looe to David's specifications for single-handed mackerel catching with room for the family. She was 14ft 6in in length, powered by a Stuart Turner engine, and carried two oars, a boat hook, an anchor, lifebelt, flares, a hand pump, and was painted in RNLI colours.

The boat was used heavily for fishing, but was always available for rescue work, should the need arise. From 1959 until the arrival of the first inshore lifeboat, Maid M rescued one person, was involved in six searches, one standby and the recovery of one body. As David recalled, 'So the need [for an ILB] was proved without doubt

and the next step followed when I moved to Port Isaac in March 1963, back to my home village.' He then became heavily involved in setting up the station, facing questions such as 'what do we want a rescue boat here for?' There were fifteen working boats going about their fishing and the view was that they looked after each other.

With the RNLI ready to supply an inshore rescue boat, a building to house it had to be found. Space in the 'boathouse' near the beach, owned by the Council and leased to the Port Isaac Fishermen Ltd, was found and the boat was stored in their 'smelly premises', as David described them, adding, 'It was of course a temporary measure but lasted eighteen years.' When the ILB arrived, it could not get in as the beam of the trailer was greater than the width of the doors. But the council workmen arrived the next day and sorted the problem out. David recalled the event: 'We were in! What had we got? Having spent nothing, we had a telephone shelf with a message pad, a hose and tap, four hat pegs, a bench and duck board.' Such was the rudimentary nature of the first inshore rescue boat facilities.

Honorary Secretary Ray Harris had to set up a crew from scratch, and the following were the volunteers: Richard Barron, student; David Bolton, holiday home owner; Harold Brown, fisherman; David Castle; Mike Dingle, gardner; Ian Honey, carpenter; Dennis Knight, fishmonger; Mike Larkin, dentist; Brian Orchard, fishmonger; Richard Parson, fish farmer; Geoff Provis, police cadet; Warwick Provis, fishmonger; Jack Rowe, fisherman; Peter Rowe, fisherman; Mike Scott, builder; Dugald Sproull, solicitor; Jim Sproull, fisherman; Mark Townsend, fisherman; and William Pink, coastguard.

And so the Port Isaac inshore lifeboat station was established, ready to rescue those in need.

was their success that more stations were supplied with the craft in subsequent years, and by 1966 the number of ILBs on station had risen to seventy-two. By the 1970s, when the inflatable ILB was an established part of the RNLI fleet and the small craft were performing hundreds of rescues annually, Port Isaac had joined the growing number of stations to operate the inshore craft, which has become the workhorse of the RNLI's fleet.

The early ILBs were rudimentary inflatable boats with outboard engines. They were crewed by two or three, powered by a 40hp outboard engine, and could be quickly launched, making them ideally suited for dealing with incidents such as people cut off by the tide, swimmers drifting out to sea and surfers in difficulty. The ILBs had a top speed of twenty knots, much faster than any lifeboat in service in the 1960s. The first ILB was manufactured by RFD and the 40hp Evinrude outboard engine was sometimes very difficult to start. On board, the compass was located in the middle of the floor mattress, making things uncomfortable for the helmsman who jarred himself on it when speeding over the waves. But the boats were gradually improved, and more equipment,

A formal commissioning ceremony for the station was held on 3 September 1967 when (left) the Past President of Collumpton Rotary, R.F. Andrews, presented a commemorative plaque to the station's honorary secretary, R.M. Harris, after which the ILB was launched (right) for a demonstration.

Inshore lifeboat D-139 on service to a capsized yacht.

Memories of Dugald Sproull

Dugald Sproull, who was involved in the station at its establishment, recalled: 'I was there at the start, as was my brother Jimmy. My mother kept the RNLI going in Port Isaac from the war days until my wife, Helen, took over for a short time before the great Surgeon Captain Baskerville appeared and formed a committee to establish a branch proper. My mother and Helen organised a flag day every summer. We had a load of cardboard lifeboat collecting boxes and I remember as a young boy counting the money that had been collected. I also remember walking every year up to Trelights to collect from Boss Thomas, who then lived in Longcross. He always gave a five pound note, much more than anybody else. Throughout the 1940s and 1950s the Sproulls were the only RNLI connection in the village.' Dugald and his brother Jimmy joined the original lifeboat crew, and each served for over twenty years, for which they were awarded the RNLI's Long Service Badge in recognition of their contribution.

including VHF radio, flexible fuel tanks, flares, an anchor, a spare propeller and first aid kit, was added.

The first IRB to go on station in the West Country was sent to St Ives, to be joined in the next couple of years by inflatables at Newquay (1965), Bude (1966) and Port Isaac. The inflatable craft was found to be ideally suited to working in the heavy surf encountered off the beaches of North Cornwall, and when one came to Port Isaac for the summer of 1967 it restarted a life-saving service that had once been fulfilled by pulling lifeboats. The first inshore rescue boat (IRB), No.139, arrived on 28 June 1967. This boat was presented to Port Isaac RNLI by Cullompton (Devon) Rotarians, and was delivered to the embryonic station on the back of a lorry, with none of the formalities which heralded the arrival of the first *Richard and Sarah* ninety-eight years before.

A home was found for the inflatable in the fish cellar, the property of Port Isaac Fishermen Ltd, beside the slipway down to the beach. The boat, transported on a trolley, was manhandled

The first inshore lifeboat to serve at Port Isaac was D-139, a 15ft 3in RFD PB16 type inflatable. The two crew on board in this old postcard photograph are wearing lifejackets of a design that remained unchanged until 1997, while protective headgear for ILB crews was not issued until 1975. While many designs were tried and tested it was only in 1998 that an suitable design of helmet was found. The sophistication of twenty-first century inshore lifeboats and their equipment is a far cry from the ILBs of the 1960s and 1970s. (From an old postcard supplied by Nicholas Leach)

down to the water when the call came. During 1967, the first summer of operations, no services were undertaken, but in 1968 the boat was called out seventeen times, and four boats and five lives were saved. By the following season the boat was fitted with radio to facilitate communications with HM Coastguard, neighbouring lifeboats and RAF rescue helicopters, and the Port Isaac lifeboat was a well integrated part of the sea rescue scene on the North Cornish coast. The crew were issued with Everett suits, but these only kept out the wind; they wore over trousers and smocks and, by the time the boat had been launched, the crew was always wet up to their waists.

Port Isaac lifeboat crew circa 1975, with D-139: kneeling, left to right, Dugald Sproul, Flanagan, Peter Rowe and David Bolton; standing, left to right, Ted Childs, Andrew Bolton, Barry Slater, David Castle, Neville Andrews, Bob Young, Clive Martin, Mark Provis, Ian Honey, Peter Kempster and Chris Key. (By courtesy of Port Isaac RNLI)

At this period the active crew were: Richard Barron, David Bolton, Harold Brown, David Castle, Mike Dingle, Ian Honey, Dennis knight, Mike Larkin, Brian Orchard, Richard Parsons, Geoff Provis, Warwick Provis, Jack Rowe, Peter Rowe, Mike Scott, Dugald Sproull, Jim Sproull, Mike Townsend, Dr. W. Baird (Honorary Medical Officer), W. Pink (Chief Coastguard), Surgeon Commodore F.W. Baskerville CBE RN (Chairman), G. Moth (Hon Treasurer), and the Honorary Secretary was R.M. Harris.

Typical of the kind of incidents to which the first ILB was called was that on 7 July 1969. At 7.25pm the coastguard informed the honorary secretary that a yacht had fired red flares about five miles west-north-west of the station. At 7.49pm the IRB was launched in a moderate north-westerly wind with a calm sea. The IRB and her crew soon came up with the yacht *Minoru*, which had five people on board. The yacht had run out of fuel and was drifting dangerously towards the shore. The IRB stood by the yacht to await

the arrival of the Padstow lifeboat *James and Catherine Macfarlane*, which had launched at 7.50pm to help. The offshore lifeboat took *Minoru* in tow to Padstow, and the IRB returned to her station at 9pm, with the Padstow lifeboat getting back at 11.15pm.

Another incident involving not only Port Isaac and Padstow lifeboats but also the lifeboats from Bude and Clovelly took place on 22 August 1969. At 9.40am the coastguard informed the Bude honorary secretary that distress flares from a large white boat had

Jack Rowe's recollections of the 1960s

Jack Rowe, now in his 80s, was a fisherman out of Port Isaac for a long time, following in the footsteps of his father. He first worked as a solo lobster and crab fisherman from an 18ft Dory but later fished jointly with his brother, Peter, working from a larger custom built fishing boat. Peter served in the original lifeboat crew in 1967, and Jack served as crew for ten years. This is one of the rescues in which he was involved:

'As the maroon cracked off over the village I ran down and arrived at the boathouse with several others. Mike Scott and Dugald Sproull were detailed to crew with me. The callout was to find a trawler that was on fire about four miles off Boscastle. The sea had really got up with a fresh north-westerly wind and white water everywhere.

When getting the boat off the trailer, which we had to manhandle out of the station, down the slip and out onto the beach to launch, we got soaked up to the neck (no dry suits in those days). We all jumped on board, Dugald taking the helm, myself midships and Mike Scott as Bowman.

'The engine fired up and we roared out of the harbour, with Mike holding on as best he could. I could see it was going to be a hellish trip, and it was. Mike Scott kept falling back onto me as Dugald pushed the boat hard through the mounting sea, so most of the time we were airborne and bouncing around like pebbles in a bucket. There was no floor cushioning, so the knees took a real beating.

'After quite a while we sighted the trawler, which was well on fire. Although we had a radio, we had no training in the best operational use of it, and the noise of the sea and engine, and the abrupt movement of the boat, made it almost impossible to talk. So with great difficulty, I managed to pick up a message from our local Coast Guard Officer, George Gates, advising us to 'stand down', as the crew of the trawler had already been taken off by another fishing boat. You can imagine our feelings – what a let down.

'We surfed all the way home and the next day Mike Scott and I, who were near retiring age for the crew, found ourselves to be badly bruised, and black and blue, and feeling like we had been in a boxing ring. At this point in our RNLI careers, we decided for the better part of glory it was the right time to stand down from crew.'

been seen two miles west of Lower Sharpnose point. The Bude IRB was launched five minutes later in a fresh north-westerly wind with a moderate sea and a slight swell, and a helicopter was also sent to help with the search. The Clovelly lifeboat *Charles H. Barrett (Civil Service No. 35)*, on passage to Ilfracombe, was alerted at 9.50am, but the alert was cancelled and she returned to Clovelly at 2.10pm. Meanwhile, the Bude IRB found the motor cruiser *Mervic*, which had engine failure and was now under way again but was taking in water. At the request of the master, the IRB stood by *Mervic* and her crew of four, whose engine room was flooded. When she was a mile and a half north-east of Port Isaac, the engine failed again, so Port Isaac IRB was launched, putting out at 12.12pm, to relieve the Bude IRB, and Padstow lifeboat *James and Catherine Macfarlane* was also launched at 12.55pm. The lifeboat reached *Mervic* at about 2pm and took her in tow, while Bude IRB, which had run short of fuel, was beached at Port Isaac at 1pm. Port Isaac IRB returned to station at 2pm after assisting the motor cruiser, which the Padstow lifeboat towed into Padstow at 3.45pm, returning to her station an hour later.

Bullocks over cliff

Since the reopening of the station in 1967, the Port Isaac lifeboat volunteers have undertaken several remarkable and noteworthy rescues, and the following accounts describe some of these. One of the first of the noteworthy rescues was that to some stranded bullocks on 5 October 1975. The Honorary Secretary received

D-139 standing by on 5 October 1975 while an attempt was made to rescue bullocks which had fallen down cliffs at Port Quin, while policemen and the farmer's sons attempt to calm and control the animals. With an incoming tide, time was against the rescuers. (By courtesy of the RNLI)

a request from HM Coastguard at 4.06pm for the ILB to be launched to stand by teams attempting to rescue the bullocks, a number of which had fallen down a cliff into a small cove at Port Quin. Attempts to save the animals had been going on since late morning but, with the rising tide and worsening sea conditions, waves had started to break over the rescuers and there was danger that they might be washed under by the ground sea. The ILB was launched at 4.10pm and stood by until all those taking part were off the cliff.

The thirty bullocks had stampeded over the 150ft cliff during the late morning and the CG Land Rover arrived on the scene at 12.10pm to find that the farmer's sons and two policemen were at the foot of the cliffs with the animals. Port Isaac Cliff Rescue Company, including four ILB crew members, arrived at 12.55pm and laid out cliff lines and stakes and took a hawser down over the cliff. Fifteen of the bullocks were killed by their fall, five were injured and were put down by the veterinary surgeon, leaving ten to be rescued.

A helicopter arrived at 2.20pm, but the pilot could not lift the cattle because of their position in the cove. Ten minutes later the East Cornwall Mine Rescue Team, who had also been called, were rigging their hawser and frame and the lift began. At 5.20pm one bullock swam out to sea, and the ILB crew managed to get a line around its neck, with crew Member Harry Pavitt lassoing it at his first attempt. However, it was not possible to tow the animal so it was released; it swam off again and was drowned. In the end, five bullocks were successfully hauled to the top of the cliff, the others being overtaken by the incoming tide and severe ground swell. The ILB left the cove at 6.07pm, when all the rescuers were off the cliff, and returned to station ten minutes later.

For this service Port Isaac ILB station and Port Isaac Cliff Rescue Company were awarded certificates of merit by the Royal Society for the Prevention of Cruelty to Animals. The crew members in the Cliff Rescue Company were Clive Martin, Ian Honey, Edwin Flanagan and David Castle. The ILB was crewed by Robert Carter, Mark Provis and Harold Pavitt.

The Pebble Mill Dash

In 1972, to mark fifty years of broadcasting, BBC TV Pebble Mill studios at Birmingham promoted what became known as The Pebble Mill Dash, inviting competitors from all parts of the country to travel to the studios by the most original method they could devise. So Port Isaac Chairman, David Castle, and two of the crew, Robert Carter and Roy Cave, decided to take up the challenge with the aim of raising funds for the Cornish Lifeboat Appeal to provide new lifeboats for Falmouth and Sennen Cove.

Their plan was to take an inshore lifeboat from Port Isaac by sea, canal and river to Pebble Mill in Birmingham. This ambitious project involved 240 miles of travel over four days starting by heading up the North Devon coast, with stops at Clovelly, and then into the Bristol Channel, calling at Minehead and Weston-super-Mare lifeboat stations to take on fuel. From Bristol a course was set for Birmingham using the river Severn and then the Sharpness Canal to reach Gloucester, then up the Severn to Tewkesbury and Worcester, where they joined the Worcester-Birmingham canal for the final leg.

At Selly Oak they were met by a trailer to transport them the last half mile by road to Pebble Mill. Their inland waterway passage into the heart of England involved negotiating a sixty locks and navigating four tunnels, one of which was more than two miles long. On reaching the studios the crew presented the Lord Mayor of Birmingham with an illuminated scroll containing greetings from the Chairman of Cornwall County Council, offering a warm welcome to the citizens of Birmingham who holidayed in Cornwall, and to encourage support the Cornish Lifeboat Appeal.

In November 1972, three crew from Port Isaac, lead by David Castle, took up the challenge to take their lifeboat from Cornwall to Birmingham by sea and canal, something that involved negotiating no fewer than sixty locks and four tunnels, one of which was two miles long, to take part in the BBC Pebble Mill Dash celebrating fifty years of broadcasting and bid for the prize to help fund new lifeboats for Falmouth and Sennen. (By courtesy of Port Isaac RNLI)

Radio and TV personality Roy Castle judged the entries, aided by hundreds of cards sent in by listeners and viewers, and joint top prize was awarded to Port Isaac RNLI and the East Midlands Sky Diving Centre, who dropped in from a helicopter. Each team received £125, presented at the evening celebrations attended by 600 people at Pebble Mill Studios, ending what was a major fund-raising effort which gave great publicity for the RNLI.

On the edge of the surf

A small boat in trouble just outside the surf at Polzeath, six miles west of Port Isaac, was reported to the honorary secretary by HM Coastguard at 5.51pm on 30 May 1976. It was overcast, with visibility about four miles, there was a fresh south-westerly breeze and the sea was moderate. At 5.54pm the ILB was launched and soon reached the casualty, the 13ft dory *Yukkie* with two people on board, at 6.18pm. Meanwhile, the yacht *Mandriella*, which had gone to *Yukkie's* assistance, found herself in difficulties as her steering linkage had parted. There was a heavy swell running and both boats were within minutes of being enveloped in the surf. Fortunately another vessel, *Tri-Star* of Padstow, was in the vicinity and went to the help of *Mandriella*, taking her in tow and leaving the ILB free to take *Yukkie* in tow. Both boats were towed to Rock, where their crews were landed, and the ILB returned to station, being rehoused at 7.49pm.

Thanks on Vellum service

A particularly fine service was carried out on 4 May 1977. A man, apparently seriously injured and lying at the foot of the cliff at Jackets Point, three miles north east of Port Isaac ILB station, was

reported to the Honorary Secretary by HM Coastguard at 1.32pm, and within ten minutes the ILB had launched. On arrival off Jackets Point, the crew could, at first, see no sign of the man but, approaching the point from the north east, a narrow entrance between the rocks became apparent in which the casualty could be seen, with people standing on the cliff tops above. The weather was fine, the wind light from the east-north-east and the tide was just starting to flood. There was little sea but a considerable swell was creating heavy breaking surf in the entrance to the cove.

Helmsman Clive Martin made a slow approach, avoiding the submerged rocks in the mouth of the cove, and, at the same time, keeping enough way on the ILB to avoid being overwhelmed by the breaking surf. After safely negotiating the entrance a sharp turn was made to starboard, the ILB was beached on the rocks close by the casualty, and the crew climbed over to where he lay. He had slipped while climbing, falling 50ft, and it was apparent that at least one of his ankles was broken and his back was injured. A Neil Robertson stretcher was lowered by the Coastguard and, while Helmsman Martin and his crew, Barry Slater and John Coshall, rendered first aid, two other Port Isaac crew members, Edward Flanagan and Andrew Bolton, climbed down the cliff. They helped to strap the casualty firmly in the stretcher and, with great care, carry him over the rocks to the ILB.

With the two extra crew members providing useful additional ballast, the ILB was successfully relaunched into the surf. Helmsman Martin followed, as closely as possible, the track successfully used to enter the cove and, handling the ILB with great skill, not only succeeded in negotiating the very heavy surf safely, but also caused no undue discomfort to the casualty. The ILB returned to Port Isaac at 2.40pm to be met by the Honorary Medical Adviser and an ambulance. On arrival at hospital, the casualty was found to have two broken ankles and a broken wrist as well as an injured back, but he was extremely grateful to the RNLI team at Port Isaac for their assistance. In recognition of their efforts during this service, the Thanks of the Institution inscribed on Vellum was accorded to Helmsman Clive Martin. Vellum service certificates were presented to crew members Barry Slater, John Coshall, Edward Flanagan and Andrew Bolton.

New inshore lifeboat D-257

In March 1978 a new inshore lifeboat was sent to the station, number D-257, funded by the Round Tables of Cornwall and Isles of Scilly. She was a Zodiac Mk.II craft, similar in size to the station's first ILB, but with an improved layout, and was formally dedicated at the station on 26 March 1978. She served for a decade and during her first summer was involved in another Vellum service. On 14 August 1978 two people in the sea at Rocky Valley, Bossiney, near Tintagel, six miles from Port Isaac, were seen to be in difficulty by HM Coastguard. Maroons were fired at 1.28pm and three minutes later the ILB was launched, setting out at full speed. Helmsman Mark Provis was accompanied by crew members Edward Fletcher and Andrew Walton. The wind was south-west, moderate force four, and a swell of ten feet and more was coming from the west.

After an uncomfortable passage lasting twenty-four minutes, the ILB arrived on scene at 1.55pm to find that a boy had been hauled out of the water by visitors on the cliff above, using a line and Kapok dumbell float. He was now on a narrow, sloping ledge underneath an overhang of rock, just above the level of the highest swells. A helicopter from RAF Chivenor was standing by to seaward, unable to effect a rescue because of the overhanging rock. Helmsman

Provis decided to anchor and veer down under oars. However, the backwash was so strong that it was not possible to row against it and so the ILB had to be taken astern on her engine to within two feet of the cliff. Crew member Fletcher jumped for the rock, but was unable to hold on and fell back into the sea, dropping into a falling swell. The next wave carried him up to the ledge ten feet above and he was able to land just below the boy.

The ILB was thrown broadside on to the rocks but crew member Walton, who was manning the radio, was able to pull her clear on her anchor cable. Meanwhile, Fletcher climbed to the boy, who was in a state of severe shock with lacerations to his hands and feet. He said his father was in the water and drowning. Edward Fletcher shouted this information to the ILB and Andrew Walton relayed it to the helicopter and Coastguard mobile, but there was no sight of the man. Edward then tried to coax the boy down the sloping ledge to where he could more easily get him into the ILB, but the boy appeared unable to move on his own.

The dedication ceremony for D-257, the second ILB at Port Isaac, in March 1978. The ILB was funded by Round Tables of Cornwall and Isles of Scilly.

Mark Provis served as a volunteer crew for more than twenty-six years, during which period the lifeboat rescued 105 lives. He was accorded the Thanks of the Institution inscribed on Vellum for a service on 14 August 1978 (By courtesy of Port Isaac RNLI)

Helmsman Provis brought the ILB close to the cliff again and crew member Walton threw the painter. But the boy was still being held fast by the line to the visitors on the cliff top, so Fletcher shouted to them to pay out the whole rope, but only about ten feet was veered. This was eventually taken by Helmsman Provis who decided to cut it and hold on to the end attached to the boy. Two large swells in succession then nearly swept Edward Fletcher and the boy into the sea and, as the ILB was carried away at the same time, Helmsman Provis had to let go the rope to avoid dragging them off the rock. Once again Helmsman Provis brought the ILB close to the rocks and this time Edward Fletcher pushed the boy into the ILB as she rose with the swell. He was safely caught by Andrew Walton and Fletcher followed, just managing to land on the ILB's sponson to be pulled aboard by Helmsman Provis.

Andrew Walton wrapped the boy in the polythene exposure sheet and the ILB headed seawards to rendezvous with the helicopter. The boy was winched into the helicopter and the ILB then searched for his father until 3.15pm, at which point the search was called off. On the passage back to Port Isaac, the ILB was diverted to Delabole Point to help in the recovery of a dead man. She stood by while the Cliff Rescue Team recovered the body, and

Senior Helmsman and Training Officer Andy Walton (left), a builder by trade, logged 200 shouts in his twenty-two years of voluntary service to Port Isaac RNLI. Senior Helmsman, fisherman and publican Neville Andrews (right) logged well over 100 shouts in his voluntary service to Port Isaac RNLI having joined the crew in 1970; he served twenty-three years, receiving a long service medal on 6 June 1990. His grandson Jack is a serving member of the current lifeboat crew.

The two senior crew members who rescued the yachtsman off Gull Rock in May 1987. Neville Andrews is in the water with Mike Daly at the helm.

then returned to station, arriving at 5.50pm, having been at sea for more than four hours. For this difficult and challenging service, the Thanks of the Institution Inscribed on Vellum were accorded to Helmsman Mark Provis and crew member Edward Fletcher. A Vellum Service Certificate was presented to Andrew Walton.

Abandoned yacht

In May 1987 Port Isaac ILB, crewed by Neville Andrews, Mike Daly and David Sumner, was launched following a reported sighting of a red distress flare seaward of Tintagel Head. Padstow lifeboat was also launched, and helicopters from RAF Chivenor and Bawdy and the coastguard mobile unit from Boscastle were alerted. The local boat Boy John, which was fishing in the vicinity, helped with the search of the area. Weather conditions were clear, but with darkness falling and a force six north-westerly wind, sea

On 8 August 1987 two anglers, cut off by the tide when they clambered to remote rocks north of Hole Beach were picked up by the ILB, which had been alerted by Hartland Coastguards. The alarm was raised at 4.31pm, after the casualties had been seen waving a red bait box to attract attention. The ILB was rehoused and ready for service at 5.35pm, having landed the pair unharmed at Port Isaac. (By courtesy of Alan Kogerson)

The 19th Annual art exhibition was opened by Jill Dando, who was working as a presenter for BBC South West, at the Port Gaverne Hotel in April 1989. David Castle, Chairman of Port Isaac RNLI, was a central figure in the art exhibitions, and he is pictured with Lt Commander Mike Lawrence, Officer Commanding 771 Squadron RNAS Culdrose, who is pointing out finer details of rig on one of the 120 paintings on show.

conditions were worsening, calling for careful handling of the ILB

Two hours after receiving the alert, a helicopter crew sighted a small rubber dinghy off Gull Rock. The ILB made for the dinghy, and took the casualty on board. The return passage was lively in difficult sea conditions, but once back at Port Isaac the casualty was examined by medical officer Doctor Jim Lunny, who established that the person was suffering from hypothermia but otherwise unhurt. The casualty was a forty-five-year-old sailor from Liverpool who had abandoned his yacht after it started to fill with water and drifted for eight hours with the engine immobilised while he was on passage from Liverpool to Gibraltar. When the yacht started to sink, he had no choice but to abandon ship. With the conditions

Television presenter Jill Dando, as a friend of Port Isaac lifeboat station, supported the fund raising activity by visiting the Griffin Inn in Brentford to meet publicans Simone and Bob Dolan, who were regular visitors to the village and supporters of the lifeboat. Each year they set up a gallon whiskey bottle on their bar in which customers were invited to make donations. In this photograph Jill has just cracked open the bottle, releasing nearly £500 of coins to be donated to Port Isaac lifeboat. (By courtesy of Port Isaac RNLI)

The inshore lifeboat speeding
in towards Cartway Cove,
to the east of Port Gaverne.
(By courtesy of the RNLI)

as they were, he was fortunate to be located and rescued before attempting to land in the small rubber dinghy in the notorious area of Gull Rock, Trebarwith

On 12 July 1987 the station celebrated twenty years of ILB service with a service held at St Peter's Church, conducted by Father Hugh Fryer, Chaplain to the station, and attended by more than 150 people. At the time, the crew were 'trained in seamanship, communications, coastal knowledge, medical aid and resuscitation, including working with helicopters. At present there are seventeen members on the crew list, and they include fishermen, a builder and decorator, a nursing officer, an electronics engineer, a grocer, a butcher, a dentist and a solicitor'. Between 1967 and 1987 the ILB had launched 252 times on service and saved 136 lives. The

For five nights during November and December 1987 crew members attended classes in one of the RNLI's specially equipped mobile units which travelled visited stations round the country. The course was run by Staff Instructor David Harvey, and covered radio communication and an introduction to chartwork. The course was attended by crew members Nigel Andrews, John Coshall, Richard Hambly, John McDonnell, Mike Daly, Greg Hingley, Paul Hingley and Dr James Lunny. (By courtesy of Port Isaac RNLI)

majority of the calls were to boats in trouble, with cliff incidents the next most numerous rescue.

D-366 Peter and Mollie Tabor

On 15 June 1988 the third inshore lifeboat to serve at Port Isaac, number D-366, was declared operational. Named *Peter and Mollie Tabor*, she was funded through the gift of Peter and Mollie Tabor, of Glastonbury, Somerset. The new ILB was dedicated at a service held in October 1988, when the boat was formally handed over to Lt Commander Jeremy Tetley, a vice-president of the RNLI, before being handed to Honorary Secretary David Castle. Station chaplain Father Hugh Fryer and Methodist Minister John Young conducted the service of dedication, and flowers were presented to Mrs Tabor by six-year-old Emily Walton, daughter of crew member Andy Walton. Music was provided by St Breward Silver Band and the Port Isaac Singers. Following the service, there was a flypast by a Sea King helicopter from RNAS Culdrose displaying the RNLI flag and the ILB was launched, crewed by John Coshall, Nigel Andrews and Greg Hingley.

In July 1987 the station marked twenty years of inshore lifeboats with a service of dedication, which was attended by more than 150 people. Pictured are some of the ILB crew and their wives following the service, with the inscribed bibles gifted by the Gideon Society for the occasion; they are, front, left to right, John Scott (Station Press Officer), Carole Provis, Jill McDonnell, Anne Sumner, Enid Andrews, Lesley Walton and Dr Jim Lunny; back row, left to right, Mike Larkin, John McDonnell, John Coshall, Harry Pavitt (behind), Marion Andrews, Nigel Andrews, John Brown, Paul Hingley, Richard Hambly and Greg Hingley. (By courtesy of Port Isaac RNLI)

D-366 *Peter and Mollie Tabor* spent nine years at the station, and was involved in numerous incidents and rescues. On occasions the Port Isaac lifeboat crew worked with lifeboats and crews from neighbouring stations and such was the case on 30 May 1995, when three lifeboats were involved in a search for survivors after the 137-year-old sailing ship *Maria Asumpta* foundered, running ashore on the rocky North Cornwall coast, having left Gloucester Docks on 27 May 1995 after a major refit and survey. The ship, believed to be the oldest sailing vessel afloat, was entering the Camel estuary in a fresh north-westerly breeze when she hit rocks on the eastern side of the entrance, near Rumps Point. The crew attempted to use the engines to pull the vessel clear, but within five minutes of them being started they stopped without warning. More sail was set, but to no avail and the ship was gradually pushed towards the rocks, which she hit without the crew able to do anything. She began to break up almost immediately, with people watching from the cliffs as the doomed ship started to go to pieces within minutes, in a scene which must have been played out a century earlier when wooden sailing ships were the norm.

Padstow's 47ft Tyne class lifeboat *James Burrough* was launched at 4.37pm from just across the estuary, by when D-366 *Peter and Mollie Tabor* had been afloat a couple of minutes, crewed by Andy Walton, Richard Hambly and Paul Worden, undertaking the three-mile passage to the scene. Both lifeboats were on scene within thirty minutes, but there was little to be done as the vessel

D-366 Peter and Molly Tabor on exercise. D-366 differed from other ILBs as she had additions to the canopy as requested by the Port Isaac crew. She was powered by a single 40hp outboard engine giving her a speed of twenty-three knots, and normally carries a crew of three. Her equipment included a VHF radio, first-aid kit, flares, anchor, compass and flexible fuel tanks. (By courtesy of the RNLI)

The service of dedication for D-366 Peter and Mollie Tabor took place in October 1988. Pictured handing over the boat is RNLI Regional Manager Andrew Young. Honorary Secretary David Castle accepted the boat and is sitting next to the Rev John Young. Father Hugh Fryer and the Rev John Young led the service of dedication. Sitting behind is Chairman Annie Price. Between 1967 and the naming of D-366 in 1988, the Port Isaac lifeboats had launched 280 times and rescued 146 people. (By courtesy of the RNLI)

had gone to pieces very quickly. Of the fourteen people aboard, all but three were picked up by fishing vessels or climbed the cliffs of the point before the lifeboats arrived. A helicopter recovered the body of one person from the casualty, while both lifeboats searched fruitlessly for the other two people who were missing. The search lasted until nightfall – both lifeboats leaving the area after 9pm – but only wreckage was recovered.

The search was resumed the following day in slightly calmer conditions, when the Padstow and Port Isaac lifeboats were joined by the D class inshore lifeboat from Rock, then newly-established, a few miles further up the estuary. However, once again only wreckage and personal effects were recovered. The final death toll following the loss of this historic vessel was three. Those who lost

D-366 Peter and Molly Tabor with Port Isaac lifeboat crew in 1995. (By courtesy of Port Isaac RNLI)

their lives were Anne Taylor, the ship's cook; Emily Macfarlane, the assistant bosun, aged nineteen from Felixstowe; and twenty-four-year-old John Shannon, the second engineer, from Australia.

The tragedy had unfolded in full view of onlookers and the repercussions which followed were considerable. In the immediate aftermath some people looted the remains of the vessel, with police making two arrests, while the Department of Transport launched two investigations into the events. These took more than two years to fully report and conclusions to be reached, culminating in a trial at Exeter Crown Court in August 1997 which found Mark Litchfield, owner and master of *Maria Asumpta*, guilty of the manslaughter of the three crew who died. He was found to have ignored adverse winds and tides, sailed the ship too close to the shore to enable spectators to see her, and taken on contaminated fuel which blocked filters and caused the engines to fail. It was a sad end to a tragic event which was widely reported nationwide.

At 3.35pm on 27 October 1996 two persons were reported to be cut off by the tide on rocks at Port Gaverne and five minutes later the maroons were fired. The crew got kitted up and the DLA gave the authority to launch, and he then assisted in launching the ILB into rough seas. The ILB soon arrived at Port Gaverne and

Inshore lifeboat D-366 Peter and Mollie Tabor on exercise, crewed by, left to right, Richard Hambly, John McDonnell and Andy Walton. (By courtesy of the RNLI)

Above: The historic sailing ship Maria Asumpta going ashore on rocks near Padstow, 30 May 1995.

Right: Eleven of the fourteen people on board Maria Asumpta managed to save their own lives, but one crew member was washed away and two were drowned while trying to swim to safety. The wooden vessel went to pieces in minutes after coming ashore on the treacherous rocks of North Cornwall's unforgiving coast.

Port Isaac ILB crew search the wreckage and remains of Maria Asumpta, May 1995. (Maria Asumpta images supplied by Bob Bulgin)

Above: The historic sailing ship Maria Asumpta in happier times. The brig measured 125ft overall, 24ft in beam and was of 127 gross tons. She was fitted with two engines, but was usually sailed, and could reach nine knots under sail.

Above left: The Daily Telegraph for 8 August 1997 reporting the outcome of the trial at which the master of Maria Asumpta was found guilty of manslaughter.

found two men, who had been fishing, in a difficult position with a rising tide and heavy ground seas. A Coastguard man was above them on the cliff edge. Crewman Mike Edkins jumped onto rocks from the ILB and assisted both casualties, one by one, into the ILB, which then returned to Port Isaac with both casualties. It was reported that, immediately after the rescue, a heavy sea broke over the rock where casualties had been, and this would almost certainly have washed them into the sea. As both were in heavy clothing, and one could not swim, it is unlikely they would have survived. The speed of launch proved to be of the utmost importance in this incident, and Mike Edkins received a special letter of thanks in recognition of his role in this efficiently executed rescue.

New lifeboat house

Since the reopening of the station the D class inflatables, on their trolleys, had been kept in the fish cellar owned by Port Isaac Fishermen Ltd. While this arrangement was adequate, it was intended only as a temporary arrangement and was far from ideal.

Port Isaac Chairman, Bob Bulgin (back centre), crew, committee and station officials with the new ILB donated by Peter and Molly Tabor in 1998. (By courtesy of Port Isaac RNLI)

The fish cellars on the beach at Port Isaac, owned by Port Isaac Fishermen Ltd, were used to house the inshore lifeboat from 1967 to 1993. When the station was opened, the cellars were seen as temporary accommodation but ended up being used for sixteen years. (Nicholas Leach)

While the ILB was housed in the fish cellars, the Quad bike launch vehicle had to be kept in another harbour building. (Nicholas Leach)

In 1993 the RNLI managed to acquire the original boathouse opposite the beach. It had been used by the Slipway House Hotel, but the ground floor was given to the Institution and refitted for the ILB. A crew room was also provided, along with better changing facilities, and the volunteer crew had more space and better accommodation in which to operate.

The refurbished building was officially opened on 26 June 1994. Miss Annie Price, chairman of the lifeboat station, welcomed the guests and invited the station honorary secretary David Castle to outline the history of the station. Following a service of dedication conducted by the station chaplain, Michael Bartlett, the guest of honour, Group Captain Simon Coy OBE RAF, commanding officer RAF St Mawgan, cut the tape and officially opened the boathouse. Music was provided by the St Breward Silver Band, which has been associated with the lifeboat station for 100 years. Between the station reopening in 1967 and the move to the boathouse in 1994, the ILBs had launched 414 times, saving 213 lives.

Top: The lifeboat station with the crew of 1989. Back row, left to right: Station Medical Officer Dr J. Lunny, lifeboat house keeper C. Hester, C. Scott, M. Provis, Neville Andrews, John Brown, John Collins, Nigel Andrews and Honorary Secretary David Castle. Front row, left to right: Richard Hambly, Steve Hunspith, John Coshall, Andy Walton, Mike Daly and John McDonnell. (By courtesy of the RNLI)

Middle: HRH The Duke of Kent meeting Port Isaac lifeboat crew in July 1990. Being introduced by Honorary Secretary David Castle are Jack Spry (deputy launching authority), and crew members Neville Andrews, Clive Martin, Richard Parsons and Harry Privitt outside the lifeboat station. (By courtesy of the RNLI)

Bottom: Honorary Secretary David Castle with newly appointed Branch Chairman Annie Price in 1993. Annie served in that capacity until 2005. Annie had spent seven months in 1982-83 filming wildlife on the South Atlantic Island of South Georgia as photographic assistant to wildlife film maker Cindy Buxton. In March they were caught up in the Argentinian invasion of the Falkland Islands, and for four weeks were trapped in a tiny hut on the edge of a glacier on South Georgia before being rescued by HMS Endurance. The presenters wrote a book about their experiences, Survival South Atlantic, and this photograph shows Annie presenting a copy to Honorary Secretary David Castle. (By courtesy of Port Isaac RNLI)

The lifeboat house, built in 1927, pictured in 1995 shortly after it had been reacquired by the RNLI and converted to accommodate the D class inflatable and its launch vehicle. (Nicholas Leach)

David Castle, Hon Sec from 1975 to 1995, pictured with HRH The Duke of Kent, was later Honorary President of Port Isaac RNLI, a position he held until his death on 29 March 2014. In 1996 he was awarded the Queens Jubilee Medal marking over 40 years service to the RNLI.

D-517 Spirit of the PCS RE

On 29 May 1997 a new inshore lifeboat was placed on station at Port Isaac, D-517 *Spirit of the PCS RE*, which had been funded by Officers and Soldiers of the Royal Logistics Corp with contributions from the Regimental Association if the Royal Logistics Corp and the Trustees of the Royal Logistics Corp. The new ILB was formally named and dedicated on 13 September 1997 at the boathouse. Miss Annie Price, Chair of the Station Branch, opened proceedings and the boat was handed over by Brigadier Mike Browne, CBE, Colonel Commandant The RLC. The service of dedication was conducted by the Reverend Prebendary Michael Bartlett, of St Endellion and Honorary Chaplain to Port Isaac station. Following a Vote of Thanks proposed by Les Vipond, Divisional Inspector of Lifeboats, Captain Debbie Jones RLC named the ILB Spirit of the PCS RE.

Despite having a projected lifespan of ten years, D-517 *Spirit of the PCS RE* served the station for only just over a year. In September 1998 she was unfortunately wrecked during a difficult and dangerous service which resulted in the award of the RNLI's Thanks on Vellum to helmsman Kevin Dingle and to crew member Mike Edkins. The service, on 6 September 1998, made headline news when the two lifeboatmen became trapped in a cave and the lifeboat became a total loss. But despite the loss of the ILB, nobody was injured and the rescue was a fine example of teamwork between the emergency services, with Padstow's all-weather

Some of the crew outside the newly refurbished ILB house on 25 April 1994. They are, left to right, John Collins (24), Paul Worden (25), and Andy Walton (40). (By courtesy of the RNLI)

The renovated lifeboat house pictured in 1994, with the D class ILB being taken down onto the beach. (By courtesy of the RNLI)

lifeboat *James Burrough*, Coastguards, Auxiliary Coastguards, an RAF and a Royal Navy helicopter all playing their part.

The events began when Port Isaac's ILB was launched after the Coastguard alerted the station to a boy being swept out to sea at Bossiney, seven miles to the north-east. Although the wind was offshore and only around force three, a very big swell was running up the coast, reaching 15ft to 20ft high in places. The ILB *Spirit of the PCS RE* put out at 4.56pm, with helmsman Kevin Dingle and crew members Mike Edkins and Paul Pollington aboard, and was able to maintain full speed down the swells until having to reduce speed for the broken water off Tintagel Head. Cutting inside the Sisters rocks, the ILB reached Bossiney inside half an hour, arriving at the same time as a helicopter from RAF Chivenor.

Padstow's Tyne class lifeboat had also been launched to provide back up and was making best speed towards the scene. The swell was about 6ft high offshore, but was surging onto the rocky foreshore and breaking heavily. By now the crew knew that they were looking for two people – the boy's father having gone into

A dark and stormy night

Dave Sumner, former Port Isaac RNLI crew, recalls a service on 1 May 1987 in which he was involved: 'It was a low spring tide and the water's edge was on a far horizon as we made our way down the beach. Neville leapt into the ILB and pulled the starter chord as if it were a garotte. The engine started, and the boat surged forward, dragging us out of the water and onto the sponsons, and we headed out to sea without knowing where to go. A radio message confirmed that we were looking for someone who had fired a red flare at about 4pm, but the report was unconfirmed.

We started a search pattern and by about 6pm it was decided that we ought to have some help so the Padstow lifeboat was requested. Three or four fishing boats were also helping in our uncoordinated search. As the evening went on, the onset of hypothermia was slowly felt in our ILB. We were tired and hungry and had found nothing. Radio procedure deteriorated between the search vessels until the Coxswain of the Padstow lifeboat, the venerable Trevor England, came onto Channel 16 and shouted at the top of his voice, 'this is the Padstow lifeboat, all vessels receiving this message shut the f**k up!' The airwaves assumed a cathedral-like silence as everybody realised that we were involved in an incident in which somebody's life was at stake.

Dave Sumner, former Port Isaac RNLI crew.

A Sea King helicopter from Culdrose had been tasked to help with the search and at 9pm we were stood down. On the way home we noticed the helicopter hovering near Ottram Rock and we diverted to investigate. The helicopter's winchman was on the way down the wire, heading for a small life-raft which was just feet from the rocks. We dashed in and snatched the man from the raft seconds before he would have been consumed by the sea, and brought him back to Port Isaac, having saved someone from almost certain death.

D class inflatable D-517
Spirit of the PCS RE being
launched on exercise.
(Albert Charman-Ord,
by courtesy of the RNLI)

the water to help his son – and began to search along the rocky
shore, paying particular attention to the caves. Two caves proved to
be empty, but Ken Richards, the Port Isaac Coastguard auxiliary in
charge, identified one particular cave as a likely spot and directed
the ILB towards it from a position on the rocks.

All three crew thought they could anchor and veer down into
the cave, despite the sea conditions, and actually reached the mouth
of the cave and glimpsed the two casualties huddled at the back
when disaster struck. A large breaker bore down on the ILB, but
Kevin Dingle kicked the engine ahead to encourage the bow to

D class inflatable D-517
Spirit of the PCS RE leaving
harbour off on exercise.
(By courtesy of the RNLI)

Three photographs shpwing D class inflatable D-517 Spirit of the PCS RE returning from an exercise in August 1998, and being recovered up the beach. (Nicholas Leach)

lift, and the wave broke heavily just after the lifeboat had ridden it. The next wave was the problem: it was described as 'a wall of water' and, although Kevin kicked the engine ahead again to lift the bow, the propeller could not find any grip in the aerated water left from the first wave. The lifeboat did not lift to the sea, and a mass of solid green water washed through her with tremendous force, sweeping Kevin Dingle and Mike Edkins out over the stern.

Both men were dashed on the shore and swept into the cave. Mike Edkins was trapped for a while, wedged by his chest and back and, as the waves broke over him, he felt that he was starting to drown. Kevin Dingle was more fortunate in that he did not become wedged, but he had to make a supreme effort and use the surge of the seas to climb to relative safety inside the cave. From

D class inflatable D-517 Spirit of the PCS RE being washed down outside the lifeboat house following her return from exercise in August 1998, a month before she was wrecked on service. (Nicholas Leach)

here he was able to shout encouragement to the two casualties, who were about 30ft from him.

Meanwhile, outside the cave Paul Pollington was left alone in the lifeboat, which had dragged her anchor and was now inside the cave mouth, being thrown against the roof with great force, breaking the canopy and an oar. Paul feared that she would be washed inside the cave and crush his fellow crew members. The engine had stopped and was full of water, so Paul began to haul the lifeboat back out of the cave using the anchor warp. This took considerable effort, but he managed it and, once outside the cave, began the post-capsize drill to restart the engine.

The downdraught from the helicopter had been blowing the ILB clear of the shore, but it moved away before Paul managed to

The remains of D class inflatable D-517 Spirit of the PCS RE wedged into the cave, September 1998. (By courtesy of Port Isaac RNLI)

The remains of D class inflatable D-517 Spirit of the PCS RE at the RNLI's Inshore Lifeboat Centre at Cowes. They were subsequently donated to the Falmouth Maritime Museum, where the transom is on display. (By courtesy of the RNLI)

restart the engine and the inflatable blew round broadside to the rocks. It was obvious that she had to be abandoned and the helicopter moved in to winch Paul to safety. The ILB was washed steadily into the cave, hitting Mike Edkins with such force that it knocked him free from the rocks which had trapped him and allowing him to climb close to Kevin Dingle. The ILB began to break up, but the wreckage took some force out of the waves as they came into the cave. It was now about 6pm, and inside the cave conditions were extremely unpleasant. Mike and Kevin knew that they had to wait for the tide to recede before they could even attempt to get out, and they and the casualties had to endure fumes from the ILB's ruptured fuel tanks as well as the tremendous air pressure caused by the waves surging into the cave.

A helicopter from RNAS Culdrose and the Padstow lifeboat, the 47ft Tyne *James Burrough*, arrived at about this time, and although those ashore were convinced that it was impossible to get into the cave, it did not stop Padstow's Coxswain Alan Tarby trying to float a fender and then the small inflatable X boat down into the entrance, or the helicopter from trying to float a lifejacket in on a line. All efforts were unsuccessful, and with high water at 6.39pm and darkness falling everyone settled down for a very

anxious wait. The Tyne held station off the cave, illuminating the mouth with her searchlight, while Coxswain Tarby fought to keep her in position as close as he dared in the heavy swells. He estimated them at about 15ft high, although those ashore thought they were nearer 20ft.

The cliff rescue team started to make their preparations and positioned themselves about 150ft above the entrance, where they were joined by other Coastguards, most of the Port Isaac crew and helpers, and even the Honorary Secretary of Rock lifeboat station. Finally, at about 9.30pm the tide had fallen enough for the crew members inside the cave to help the casualties towards the inside of the entrance and for the Coastguard team to reach the outside. There was great relief when all four were brought out safely with only relatively minor injuries, and airlifted to hospital. The ILB crew were shocked, badly bruised and suffering from inhaling petrol fumes, but were discharged later that night. The casualties, ten-year old James Leeds and his father Nick, were also shocked and bruised, and were suffering from hypothermia, and Nick had a dislocated shoulder so both were detained in hospital.

A replacement ILB, D-382, was sent from RNLI headquarters and by 3am the following day the station was operating normally again, even before the wreckage of the ill-fated ILB D-517 had been recovered with the aid of the cliff rescue team. She was so severely damaged and wedged in position that she had to be cut up and dismantled before the wreckage could be removed. And on 23 November 1998 the station's old D class ILB, D-366 *Peter and Mollie Tabor*, returned to the station as a Relief ILB to serve until another new ILB had been completed.

D-546 Spirit of the PCS RE II

Exactly a year after the old ILB was written off, a new ILB, D-546, was named *Spirit of the PSC RE II* at a ceremony on 5 September

The Port Isaac crew members involved in the service on 6 September 1998 which resulted in the loss of the ILB. They are, left to right, Mike Edkins, Alan Tarby (Padstow Coxswain), Paul Pollington and Kevin Dingle. The Thanks Inscribed on Vellum were accorded to Helmsman Kevin Dingle and crew member Mike Edkins; a Letter of Thanks signed by the RNLI Chairman was sent to Paul Pollington. (By courtesy of Port Isaac RNLI)

Launching D-546 Spirit of the PCS RE II in the harbour. (By courtesy of the RNLI)

Paramedic Richard Hambly descends from a long line of Port Isaac lifeboat volunteers. He joined the ILB crew in January 1985 and became a senior helm. During twenty-nine years of active service, he took part in more than 100 services. His son Harry is the youngest volunteer crew member, continuing a long-standing family tradition.

1999, having been placed on station on 3 June 1999. Following the well-publicised events of September 1998, when D-517 had been wrecked on service, smashed to pieces against the rocks, a campaign to raise £16,000 for a replacement was launched. Television celebrity interior designers Laurence Llewelyn-Bowen, Anna Ryder Richardson and Graham Wynne decorated a marquee for a fundraising ball which raised £7,000, and the ball itself was featured in OK magazine, which also made a donation.

The new ILB was formally delivered by RNLI Vice President Air-Vice Marshall John Tetley CB into the care of Port Isaac station, and was accepted by Honorary Secretary Ted Childs. Following a service of dedication conducted by Reverend Prebendary Michael Bartlett, of St Endellion and Honorary Chaplain to Port Isaac station, Sergeant Major Paul Snape of the Royal Logistics Corps, donors of the lifeboat which had been wrecked, named the ILB.

Stag rescued after cliff plunge

On 23 April 2002 a full scale rescue operation was launched involving the RSPCA, Coastguards and RNLI after a young deer fell over an 80ft cliff, tumbling into the sea where it surfaced and proceeded to swim strongly offshore. An eyewitness account described the animal as distressed and disorientated, at first running towards the cliff edge then back towards a nearby road, but suddenly turning and plunging over the cliff edge.

The inshore lifeboat was launched and reached the animal,

Left: Three photos taken from 180ft up, looking down from the cliffs, showing the inshore lifeboat D-546 Spirit of the PCS RE II being manhandled into the surf following the rescue of a stag in April 2002. These dramatic images show the dangers and difficulties of working at the foot of the cliffs, but the type of coastal terrain to which Port Isaac's volunteers are often called. (Bob Bulgin)

Above: The young deer, which swam a quarter of a mile out to sea before ending up stranded ashore.

Below: The stag being brought up the cliffs by Roy Speakman of the local Coastguard team, with the ILB standing by below.

Over £2,000 was raised on 29 August 2002 at the Annual Lifeboat Day, an event now known as 'lifeboat larks', which is always well supported by visitors and local residents, including TV personality Laurence Lewellyn-Bowen and his wife Jackie who have a home in the village. For this event in 2002, 450 burgers, 100 home made cakes, 500 scones, four barrels of Sharp's bitter and 14 bottles of Pimms were consumed.

Crew members Damien Bolton and Jeremy Thomas explaining the capabilities of the D class ILB to students of Launceston College in August 2002 as part of the College's annual activities week, which focused on search and rescue organisations. Over two days pupils carried out different SAR activities, including planning and coordinating sea rescue scenarios. (Both photos by courtesy of Port Isaac RNLI)

which was by then swimming out to sea. It had a fine set of pointed antlers and a lively disposition so the lifeboat crew had to be cautious of potential damage to the ILB. However, with careful boathandling by the helmsman, the ILB reached the stag, which was gradually turned and shepherded back towards the mainland, eventually coming ashore at the secluded Cartway Cove, which had no road or path access. A local vet had arrived at Port Gaverne beach and the ILB sped around to collect him, returning to the cove to treat the deer. The first attempts by the vet to tranquillise the animal failed and the deer ran into a dark cave.

At this point the lifeboat crew assisted the vet and Coastguard cliff rescue personnel in sedating the deer so that it could then be recovered and lifted up the 180ft cliff by the coastguard to a waiting RSPCA Ambulance. Amazingly, other than a few cuts and scratches, the deer was no worse for wear following its ordeal. Following a check-up at RSPCA HQ at St Columb, the animal was released into the wild later in the day. With a rising tide and

The Boscastle floods 2004 • Damien Bolton's account

On Monday 16 August 2004 the two villages of Boscastle and Crackington Haven suffered extensive damage following flash floods caused by an exceptional amount of rain that fell over eight hours that afternoon. The flood in Boscastle was extensively reported, but the floods in Crackington Haven and Rocky Valley were little mentioned beyond the local news. The floods were the worst in local memory, and the Port Isaac ILB responded to the call for help. The following is Damien Bolton's account of what happened to the Port Isaac ILB.

'The Boscastle floods were amazingly surreal. I was just sitting down to a wine tasting in our family restaurant when my lifeboat pager and Dad's coastguard pager went off. We made our way to the stations on what was a clear sunny day and the village was busy with holidaymakers. I began changing and asked Phil Tidey, Hon Sec, 'what have we got?' Phil replied, 'you are tasked to multiple casualties stranded by floods at Boscastle'. 'Pardon?' was my instant reply, but Nigel Sherratt, Andy Cameron and myself put out and headed for Boscastle.

As we made our way across the bay, Nigel informed Falmouth Coastguard that we had launched on service. The Coastguard responded: 'you are tasked to reports of mass flooding and multiple casualties stranded at Boscastle Harbour; we will update you further once we have more information.' We arrived on scene at the same time as the first helicopter from 771 squadron Culdrose. As we navigated the dog leg into Boscastle, Rescue 193 was about 40ft above our heads and 40m off our bow, and they passed a message: 'Port Isaac ILB, caution, caution on your entrance to the harbour, there is debris on its way out to you'.

Our initial thoughts were that we were going to be confronted by trees and plants, but what we actually saw was a silver VW Passat with a caravan in tow. As we sat in the fast flowing water negotiating the branches, gas bottles and garden furniture, we noticed the caravan walls were moving and creating a banging noise as if people were inside trying to raise the alarm. We readied ourselves, expecting to rip open the caravan's window to reveal a family, but when we tore off the back window it revealed nothing. The banging stopped and we realized that it was just the pressure of the water inside.

This surreal adventure was to carry on for the next few hours, with car after car flying out of the harbour along with everyday items, such as washing machines, BBQs, trees and plastic seating. We searched every car and found nobody in any of them, which was a miracle. We also concluded that it would be best to buy either an Audi or VW, as they were best at bobbing round the harbour wall with hazard lights flashing and rain sensitive wipers going.

We then saw the heavens open and thunder, rain and hail stones the size of marbles fell, bouncing off our helmets, while the most amazing lightning strikes hit the cliff face. While this was all happening we kept on hearing the Sea Kings enter the harbour in turn to effect the rescue of those stranded in their houses.

Every fifteen minutes we had to exit the harbour into clean water so that the 40hp outboard would not overheat, as the water in and around the harbour was thick with mud and silt. On about the third run we heard that Bude ILB had been tasked to come and assist. As they had recently taken delivery of a new IB1 with a 50hp engine, we warned of the potential for overheating. Sadly once on scene it only took minutes for their engine to seize so we towed them out and they set anchor while we returned.

We carried on searching the cars until they stopped coming and then made our way round the corner into the main harbour to be confronted by a view that resembled a war-torn land. But as the tide continued to drop, we were no longer required on scene so Falmouth Coastguard stood us down, and we returned to station to refuel and take stock of events.

Padstow lifeboat James Burrough in the harbour with Port Isaac's famous Fisherman's Friends preparing for a publicity photo shoot relating to a recording they made for the RNLI. The well known group recorded songs to raise funds for the RNLI under the title 'Home From The Sea', with Phil Coulter's well-known piece of that name among many sea shanties and songs. Five of the Fisherman's Friends were crew on Port Isaac lifeboat. The recording of this CD was undertaken by Clovelly Recordings Ltd, well known for the high quality of its productions, and the CD was a great success, helping to raise significant funds for the RNLI. (Bob Bulgin BEM)

increasing ground sea, the ILB crew's skills were put to the test in relaunching and making safe harbour at the end of a rescue operation which lasted five hours.

On 1 June 2004 RNLI District Inspector Howard Ramm visited the station, but the planned exercise afloat was cancelled due to the rough sea conditions, with a strong northerly blowing force four. However, ten minutes after the decision had been made to cancel the

Celebrity designer Laurence Lewellyn Bowen and his wife Jackie have been great supporters of Port Isaac RNLI, and their efforts have raised several thousands of pounds. Laurence is pictured here with some of the crew and committee for a publicity photo following his donation towards production of the station's Christmas cards. (By courtesy of Port Isaac RNLI)

The station's former D class inflatable Spirit of the PCS RE II (D-546) served for ten years, and was then used for four years as a training lifeboat, before becoming a boarding boat in 2013. She was used at Appledore, where she is pictured, to take the full-time lifeboat Coxswain and Mechanic out to the all-weather Tamar lifeboat on her moorings. (Nicholas Leach)

exercise, Falmouth Cost Guard contacted the station to report that a father and his twelve-year-old daughter had been washed off of the rocks at Barras Nose and requested the ILB launch immediately.

The ILB put out with Richard Hambly, Jeremy Thomas and Nicky Bradbury on board, accompanied by the District Inspector. Owing to heavy head seas, the ILB made slow progress to the location, arriving on scene forty minutes after launching. Boscastle Coast Guard had the twelve-year-old in visual contact and she was seen to be treading water about half-a-mile offshore.

D class inflatable D-707 Copeland Bell was placed on station on 23 November 2009. She is an IB1 type boat, the latest incarnation of the inflatable inshore lifeboat, which is the workhorse of the RNLI fleet. (By courtesy of the RNLI)

The Fishermen's Friends perform at the naming ceremony of D class inflatable D-707 Copeland Bell on 13 June 2010. (Paul Richards)

Lifeboat crew at the naming ceremony of D-707 Copeland Bell on 13 June 2010. (Paul Richards)

Below: Chairman Bob Bulgin addresses the crowd during the naming ceremony of Copeland Bell. (Paul Richards)

Below right: Father John May leads the service of dedication during the naming of Copeland Bell. (Paul Richards)

With sea conditions very poor, the lifeboat crew only spotted the casualty when she was about 15m from the port bow, but in the rough seas the ILB was unable to turn immediately to the casualty. However at this point, she turned to see the lifeboat, and being completely exhausted and expecting a rescue, she could no longer tread water and began to sink beneath the waves. Realising this, a crew member jumped into the sea and swam to the casualty, lifting her above the water and supporting her until the ILB could

manoeuvre close enough to recover both. The girl was then taken to Boscastle harbour and transferred by air ambulance to hospital where she made a full recovery. Sadly her father died.

D-707 Copeland Bell

On 23 November 2009 a new inshore lifeboat, number D-707, was placed on station. An IB1 type boat, different from her predecessors despite being outwardly similar, the new ILB had a 50hp engine with electric start-up, which gave her a speed of twenty-five knots. The floor sections and transom were fabricated from composite materials, which were as strong and stiff as plywood, the material used hitherto for ILBs, but lighter and easier to maintain. The hull was made from hypalon-coated polyester which gave a more consistent boat shape and performance. A new stowage pod, designed to allow the anchor to be stowed ready-rigged for deployment, provided housing for other equipment.

The new boat was funded by the Bude Model Boat Appeal, together with other donations and gifts from Cornwall, and was formally named on 13 June 2010 at the Harbour. Bob Bulgin, Chairman of the station, opened the ceremony, with Godfrey Copeland, representing the donors, handing over the ILB to the RNLI. The ILB was accepted by Lifeboat Operations Manager Phil Tidey, and there followed a service of dedication led by Father John May, station chaplain, priest to six parishes including Port Isaac. At the end of the ceremony, Mrs Mary Copeland formally christened the new ILB, which was then launched for a short demonstration run in the harbour.

D-707 *Copeland Bell* has been used for several noteworthy rescues, and has proved herself to be a fine lifeboat in the best traditions of the Port Isaac lifeboat station. A routine exercise turned into a full scale incident for two RNLI crew volunteers

Set into the wall of the historic Fish Sheds just opposite the ILB station is an Admiral FitzRoy type mercury barometer dating back to the 1890s and still in operational condition.

from Port Isaac on 20 February 2011 when a local rowing gig capsized. At one stage they found themselves with seven other people in the D class ILB before the casualties were transferred to the Padstow all-weather lifeboat Spirit of Padstow and on again to a rescue helicopter.

RNLI volunteers Nigel Sherratt and Ian Johnson were out training in D-707 Copeland Bell when they noticed the gig, Corsair, with seven people onboard, was experiencing problems making its way past the headland of Lobber Point. The six women, who were dressed in T-shirts, were unable to get back to Port Isaac harbour because of the large swell caused by the low spring tide, so the two ILB crew went alongside and advised the team to row further out to sea away from the swell. Two of the gig crew became anxious and it was decided to transfer them ashore, bringing two experienced members of the gig club, Trevor Beare and Steve Hudspith, out to take their places, along with warm clothing and lifejackets for all onboard.

With the two gig officials on the gig and the local Port Isaac Coastguard Rescue Team monitoring the situation from the harbour, the gig made an approach but with a big swell still running, it capsized throwing all seven into the water. They were swiftly rescued by the inshore lifeboat crew. Five were then transferred to the Padstow all-weather lifeboat Spirit of Padstow, suffering from shock, cold and some minor injuries. They were then airlifted away by a search and rescue helicopter from RNAS Culdrose to the Royal Cornwall hospital at Truro, suffering from cold and shock with some cuts and bruises. The ILB crew, with the two gig team members who had been taken out to the gig, then made their way back into harbour.

In a ceremony at the Barbican in London on 23 May 2012, Damien Bolton, Nicki Bradbury and Matt Main were awarded their medals for gallantry for the rescue of Paul Sleeman from the water. Sadly, the other person in the water, Peter Sleeman, did not survive. Despite their loss, the Sleeman family described the lifeboat crew as 'truly amazing people; without their skills, bravery and determination Paul wouldn't be here today'. Linda Sleeman, widow of Peter, is a leading member of Port Isaac RNLI Committee. (By courtesy of the RNLI)

In London for the RNLI Annual Presentation of Awards in 2012, the Port Isaac with the other medal recipients on board the Tower lifeboat. Damien's Silver medal was the first that had been awarded to Port Isaac rescuers since 1870. (By courtesy of the RNLI)

Phil Tidey, RNLI Lifeboat Operations Manager at Port Isaac, says the team performed extremely well: 'The two crew did a fantastic job, monitoring the situation, transferring people, clothing and equipment, and ultimately rescuing the people from the gig. In fact they managed to get all seven people out of the water in less than five minutes. Their training really did pay off in this situation and thank goodness they were out training yesterday and were able to monitor the gig from an early stage. I would also like to thank the coastguard rescue team members who saw events from the cliff and were able to radio information about the sea conditions to the ILB crew. I must also pay tribute to the ILB herself. She performed superbly and was even able to play host to nine people at one stage, though the crew were absolutely right to transfer five of them to the Padstow all-weather lifeboat before making their own approach to the harbour.'

Helmsman Nigel Sherratt and crewman Ian Johnson were commended for their actions in effecting the rescue, and both were presented with framed Letters of Thanks from the RNLI Chief

Nicki Bradbury, Matt Main and Damien Bolton with HRH The Duke of Kent in London on 23 May 2012 after they had been awarded their medals for gallantry. (By courtesy of the RNLI)

Damien Bolton joined the lifeboat service at Port Isaac on his seventeenth birthday in July 1997. He subsequently became a senior helm and the station's training officer.

Executive Paul Boissier. Nigel came from a well-known Port Isaac family who were bakers, and his great-grandfather George Strutt served as crew on the second Richard and Sarah. Nigel joined the crew in 1999, qualified as a helmsman in 2008 and became a Deputy Launching Authority in May 2014.

Medal service of April 2012

The most outstanding rescue undertaken by the volunteer crew in D-707 *Copeland Bell*, and indeed one of the finest rescues in the history of Port Isaac lifeboat station, took place in April 2012. The ILB was launched on 8 April 2012 just after 8.25am following the receipt of reports that two people were in the water at Tregardock. On board *Copeland Bell* were volunteer helmsman Damien Bolton and crew members Nicola-Jane Bradbury and Matthew Main. The wind was west-southwest force four to five, and with high tide approaching and the wind blowing onshore, the conditions at the cliffs where the two men had been swept into the water were challenging. When the lifeboat crew arrived on scene at 8.36am, they found a three-metre dumping sea breaking onto the cliff face, exacerbated by waves reflecting off the cliff, which created a rough and confused sea close inshore.

The coastguard informed the volunteers that the two casualties were in the water at an area called The Steps and that an RAF rescue helicopter had been tasked and was eleven minutes away. Damien headed to the area and spotted two people in the water

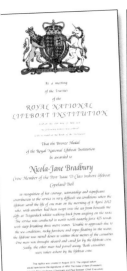

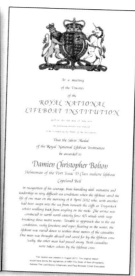

The three Medal Service Certificates that were presented to three lifeboat crew, Nicola-Jane Bradbury, Matt Main and Damien Bolton, for their outstanding service in April 2012.

Below: RNLI Bronze medal for gallantry.

very close to the cliffs, being tumbled in the surf. While he was assessing the situation, one of the casualties was turned by a wave and, on seeing the lifeboat, shouted for help and raised an arm before disappearing below the surface again.

Damien decided to veer down, a technique in which the crew pay out the anchor cable while applying astern power, manoeuvring the lifeboat backwards under control towards the casualty. By this means the crew used the anchor to help control

On 25 April 2012, at the 45th Annual General Meeting of the Branch, several awards were made to Committee Members and Station Officials in recognition of their invaluable and voluntary service to the RNLI. The ceremony was attended by Mary and Godfrey Copeland who donated a major part of the cost of the ILB which came on station in 2009. Chairman Bob Bulgin presented Deputy Launching Authority Byron Buse with a Silver Statue of a lifeboat man together with a framed certificate. Carole Raynor received a Silver Badge and framed certificate recognising twelve years of service to the branch, nine as Secretary. Sandie Bulgin was awarded a Silver Badge and framed certificate in recognition of seventeen years of service covering retail sales and events organisation. A Bronze Badge and framed certificate went to Jan Rowe for her work as Station Box Secretary. A Bronze Badge and framed certificate went to David Raynor, a key member of the Committee, and Treasurer. A Bronze Badge was also presented to Liz Cook to mark fourteen years on the committee. Pictured at the event are, left to right, Mary Copeland, Carole Raynor, Sandie Bulgin, Byron Buse, Jan Rowe, David Raynor, Liz Cooke and Godfrey Copeland. (By courtesy of Port Isaac RNLI)

D class inflatable D-707 Copeland Bell being launched for a training exercise, with Lifeboat Operations Manager Chris Bolton driving the tractor. (Nicholas Leach)

Launching D-707 Copeland Bell across the beach. (Nicholas Leach)

D-707 Copeland Bell leaving the harbour on exercise. (Nicholas Leach)

D-707 Copeland Bell on exercise. (Nicholas Leach)

Recovery of D-707 Copeland Bell after a routine exercise, with Lifeboat Operations Manager Chris Bolton driving the recovery tractor. (Nicholas Leach)

D-707 Copeland Bell is brought back to the boathouse after a training exercise. (Nicholas Leach)

A summer scene at Port Isaac, with D-707 Copeland Bell outside the boathouse and being washed down after a routine exercise. (Nicholas Leach)

the position of the lifeboat when working near a dangerous lee shore. Damien positioned the lifeboat about 70m from the casualty so that Matthew could drop the anchor and then slack the anchor warp, while Nicola-Jane kept a lookout for large waves and operated the radio. Damien helmed the lifeboat safely over two sets of three-metre waves as he brought it within three metres of the cliff face and a couple of metres from the casualties. One was holding onto the other and an orange rope appeared to be tangled around them. Concerned that the rope may get caught around the ILB's propeller if he went closer, Damien called for the men to swim to the boat.

First wrapping the line around his fellow casualty, one of the men made his way to the ILB where Nicola-Jane and Damien attempted to pull him aboard. Matthew warned that a large wave was approaching, which then broke over the lifeboat, filling it with water. At the same time, the engine stopped and the lifeboat began to turn sideways to the waves, exposing the crew to the risk of capsize. Damien quickly restarted the engine and applied power astern to turn the lifeboat's bow to face the waves. All three crew members then worked together to get the casualty on board. The orange rope was attached to him and it appeared to be connected to the man still in the water, so Matthew secured one end to the lifeboat.

With the confused seas and submerged rocks, the lifeboat and crew were operating at their limits. The casualty onboard the ILB

Lifeboat crew and station personnel with D-707 Copeland Bell outside the lifeboat house. They are, left to right, George Cleave, James Bolton, Damien Bolton, Jon Wide, Sam Eaves, Phil Tidey, Nigel Sherratt, Bob Bulgin and Chris Bolton. (Nicholas Leach)

Andy Cameron has been a volunteer with the RNLI for fifteen years, and a helm for ten years. With a commercial endorsed coastal skipper licence, he has been at sea all his life in different roles. His company, Wavehunters, sells clothing and memorabilia, offers surfing instruction, coastal tours and individually tailored sea life charters.

was deteriorating rapidly and needed immediate care, so the crew had to make a quick assessment of the situation. Having not seen any response from the second casualty, and since reaching him could put everybody on the lifeboat in more danger, Damien decided to helm the ILB away from the cliff where the first man could be transferred to the helicopter, which was on its way.

It was too risky to recover the anchor, so Matthew cut the line and Damien took the ILB towards deeper water, pulling the second casualty clear of the cliff as he did so. Once away from the cliff and out of the breaking seas, the crew attended the first casualty, who was drifting in and out of consciousness. Matthew took off his helmet and put it onto the man's head to prevent heat loss. Meanwhile, Damien pulled in the orange line to bring the second casualty alongside the ILB. Sadly, he was not breathing and was unresponsive and was later declared dead. The crew's priority was to evacuate the first casualty, whose condition was deteriorating, and they quickly manoeuvred the ILB so that he could be winched into the rescue helicopter. He was taken to hospital where he subsequently made a full recovery.

The lifeboat station, pictured in 2015, is one of focal points of the picturesque Port Isaac village, with its doors always open. (Nicholas Leach)

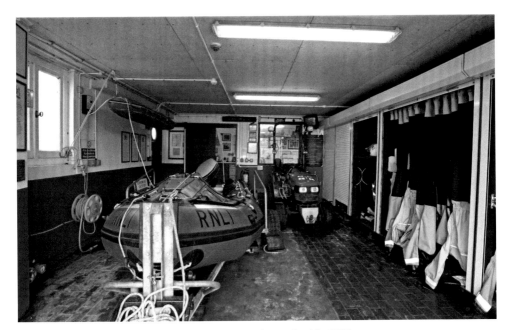

This outstanding rescue showed what the D class inflatable ILB's capabilities. Damien used great seamanship skills to manoeuvre the vessel, operating at the extreme limits of its capabilities, towards the two men, who were struggling to stay above the crashing surf. For their outstanding courage and bravery in the face of great danger, the three volunteer crew were awarded gallantry medals by the RNLI. Damien received the Silver medal, and Nicola-Jane and Matthew were each awarded with the Bronze medal. Michael Vlasto, RNLI operations director, said:

> 'This was a service carried out in very difficult conditions with confused and breaking seas very close to a dangerous lee shore, with semi-submerged rocks and floating rope in the water. Helmsman Damien Bolton and his two crew, Nicola-Jane Bradbury and Matthew Main, were aware of the risk they were exposing themselves to, but felt that the potential of saving a life outweighed that risk. Although this rescue was also tinged with tragedy, it is a testament to their bravery, skill and tenacity that one of the men survived and made a full recovery.'

Paul Sleeman, who survived the incident, and the rest of his family, said: 'Paul, Linda, Mark, Jenna, Emma and the rest of the family of the late Peter Sleeman would like to pass on their sincere congratulations to Damien, Nicki and Matt, three truly amazing people, for their very worthy awards. Without their skills, bravery and determination Paul wouldn't be here today. His life was saved with seconds to spare. Also, the huge effort they went to, to recover Pete which enabled us to lay him to rest, something that the whole family will always be grateful for. The family are also

The D class inflatable inshore lifeboat ready for the call, with the crew's dry suits hanging up, and visitors can see inside the boathouse and make a donation if they wish. (Nicholas Leach)

grateful for the continuous help and support during this tragic and difficult time from all at Port Isaac RNLI. Some wonderful, strong, long-term relationships have been made. Port Isaac RNLI now holds a very special place in all our hearts.'

On New Year's Day 2012 at 3.30pm helmsman Andy Cameron was about to celebrate with friends at the Golden Lion when his pager went off. Someone had been reported in the water between Bossiney and Tintagel Head and, with a northerly wind and strong swells, Andy knew this was going to be a tough assignment. As the casualty was already in the water, speed of response was crucial. Nicola Bradbury, one of the most experienced lifeboat women in the UK, and Matt Main, a probation helm, made up the crew.

Andy recalls the passage to the casualty: 'As we sped across Port Isaac Bay towards Bossiney we were battling two to three meter swell and a force six northerly wind but making steady progress towards Tintagel Head, where the tides and weather met, whipping up a confused sea. Once we were round the Head, the swell, which had been abeam, set to our stern so we then encountered a huge following swell.' Navy 192 Sea King helicopter had been scrambled and both Boscastle and Port Isaac Auxiliary Coastguards were en route.

Andy explains what happened next: 'We headed round to Merlins Cave, but we could see nobody on the cliffs or in the water. With the light fading, I set course through formidable swell towards Bossiney. Suddenly, on the port side, I saw something about 400m away and, once we were close enough, Matt grabbed the person and I helped haul him on board. Matt immediately

Port Isaac RNLI Committee 2016. Left to right, David Raynor (Treasurer), Sally Harvey, Liz Bolton (Deputy Chairman/Secretary), Faye Archell (Deputy Press Officer) David Pentland, Julie Monk, Carole Raynor, Chris Bolton (LOM), Linda Sleeman, Bob Bulgin BEM (Chairman), Sandie Bulgin, Cheryl Webster (Deputy Box Secretary), Jan Rowe (Box Secretary); inset Annie Price (ex-Chairman 1993-2009). (Photo by Adrian Jasper)

Chris Bolton • Lifeboat Operations Manager

The post of Lifeboat Operations Manager at Port Isaac has been held by Chris Bolton since April 2014. He took on the role following sixteen years as a dedicated helper, and fourteen years of service as a member of the Port Isaac Coastguard Cliff Rescue team. A keen power boat man and active in kayaking around the North Cornish coast, he brought a wealth of maritime experience to the operational role. Chris' two sons, Damien (senior helm and training officer) and James, are crew members and his wife Liz the station's Deputy Chairman. They follow a long-standing family tradition as the Boltons are related to the late Honorary President and one time Honorary Secretary David Castle, who also had two sons serving on the crew and his wife Kathleen on Committee. (Nicholas Leach)

started reviving the casualty, who was responsive, but totally drained, hypothermic and had clearly given up. We asked questions to keep him awake: have you been unconscious at any point? Have you inhaled water? Are you alone? He was heavily hypothermic, and although Matt did his best to keep him conscious, we needed to get him medical care immediately.

'An ambulance was waiting at Boscastle, where the entrance was going to be horrendous. But with conditions continuing to deteriorate, I was sure that we had recovered the only person in the water and the chance of finding another in the dark was minimal. So we decided to attempt to enter Boscastle. As we thought, the entrance was a nightmare, with heavy swell reflecting back off cliffs. But at full tilt, in the pitch black, surfing in at twenty knots, we managed to round the dog leg harbour walls and land the ILB, quickly offloading the casualty into the care of the ambulance medics.

'Our prop had been smashed on rocks as we sped into the harbour, so we were unable to relaunch , but it did not matter. We had saved a life. Throughout this rescue I never doubted the capability of my crew, the boat, the shore team and committee, who collectively enabled us to get the job done. This was borne out by the many letters, personal visits and donations to the RNLI made by the family following this dramatic incident.'

In 2013 a twinning arrangement was established between Welwyn Garden City & Hatfield RNLI Branch and Port Isaac RNLI. As a result, some of the funds raised by Welwyn Garden City and Hatfield were given directly towards the operational

Service board on display inside the boathouse listing the rescues performed by the pulling and sailing lifeboats. (Nicholas Leach)

Chairman Bob Bulgin receives his British Empire Medal from the Lord Lieutenant of Cornwall, Colonel Edward Bolitho OBE, on Sunday 8 June 2014. During the presentation, Damien Bolton, Senior Helm, said: 'We all hold Bob very close in our hearts, not just within the RNLI but within Port Isaac. He has been an active part of the Port Isaac lifeboat for the last eighteen years and active within the RNLI for over fifty. This is just one of several significant charities and organisations he has dedicated his spare time to and we're all very proud that he has quite rightly been recognised with the award of the BEM.' Bob was awarded the RNLI's Bronze Badge in 2003, the Silver Badge in 2009 and the Gold Badge in 2016.

commitments of Port Isaac lifeboat and crew. For several years before 2013 the Chairmen of the inland fund-raising branch and the station had been developing a good relationship, and since the twinning was formalised over £8,781 was provided to help with crew training and general maintenance and running costs of the ILB. As well as funds being provided, Port Isaac volunteer crew members went to Welwyn Garden City and Hatfield Branch to meet and talk to the committee and supporters, giving a presentation about the work of the station. This arrangement has resulted in a close bond to be formed between the two Branches.

On 20 October 2013 the ILB became stranded on a sand bar at Trebarwith Strand, near Tintagel, in Cornwall, after it capsized at around 11am. A spokesman for the Coastguard said a rescue crew from Boscastle and Port Isaac attended the scene, adding that, while it was unusual for lifeboats to capsize, conditions were treacherous with high winds and a large swell. Both lifeboat crew members ended up in the sea and swam to nearby Tregardock beach, where they were picked up. Chairman of the station, Bob Bulgin, said: 'The crew were on routine sea training. A wave caught them and capsized the boat. We have to train in adverse conditions. They are in areas that can be treacherous because it is where they have to carry out rescue operations. No one was hurt, they followed all the correct procedures. They were fine after their ordeal.' The boat was

The three station and committee awards also presented by Lord Lieutenant Colonel Edward Bolitho OBE on Sunday 8 June 2014 were to, left to right: Phil Tidey, engineer and Lifeboat Operations Manager to 2014; Cheryl Webster, Assistant Box Secretary; and Christine Clifton, Fund-raising Committee Secretary.

Crew members enjoy a fish supper at Nathan Outlaw's Fish Kitchen on 2 October 2015 support of the RNLI's Fish Supper campaign to raise funds for the charity. The restaurant has been a strong supporter of the Port Isaac crew, ten of whom enjoyed a selection of fish dishes for their lunch. (RNLI/ Simon Culliford)

A difficult search • Matt Main's account

On 22 January 2014, a wild, windy and wintery day, Port Isaac was extremely quiet . . . until my pager sounded at 9.40am. I quickly made my way to the station, and was there within half a minute to be met by DLA Phil Tidey, who told me that a man has been washed from the rumps while fishing and was in the water. He was with another person who was safe and keeping an eye on his fishing buddy. We made the boat ready and waited for crew.

Mark Grills was next to arrive and, after briefing Mark, I decided to launch with just the two of us, knowing that Rock ILB and Padstow ALB had also been called out and a person in the water at that time of year would not survive long. The sea state was very confused, with large cresting waves from all directions, and we could only average twelve knots across Port Isaac Bay, past Port Quin and on to the rumps. Rescue 193 helicopter from RNAS Culdrose had also been tasked and two land-based coastguard teams were helping. We were the first on scene and immediately started a shore line search from where the casualty had entered the water.

Due to the rebounding sea it was unsafe to get within fifty yards of the cliff face. We found a rucksack with fishing tackle in it, and a minute later we found a woollen hat. At this point Rock ILB came on scene, so both ILBs undertook sector searches. About five minutes later Rescue 193 arrived, and, as the helicopter came into view over Trevose Head, Rock ILB radioed that they had found the casualty. We saw that they were pointing at a casualty, face down in the water, about twenty-five yards away, but as the visibility was so bad in the water we lost sight of him. Rescue 193 maintained visual contact with the casualty and lowered a winchman, but we lost visual contact and, despite putting an orange smoke canister in the water to mark the last known position, we could not find the casualty.

Padstow ALB arrived on scene, and crewman Stephen Swabey from the ALB was transferred to our boat as a third crewman as I felt that it would be advantageous to the search efforts. All assets then searched for four hours from the rumps to Stepper Point and around Newland Island, with the sea increasing in size throughout. We were unable to get within fifty yards of Newland as the bigger set waves where breaking over the island. Rescue 193 had to go to Newquay airport to refuel mid search, and as we were also running low on fuel, returned Padstow's crewman, and returned to Port Isaac. The 22 year old man from Plymouth was never found, and my thoughts often go to the family of that man.

Matt Main joined the crew in 2006, on leaving the Royal Engineers, and successfully completed the helmsman course at the Lifeboat College in Poole.

largely undamaged, but a replacement engine was brought from RNLI headquarters in Poole, and was fitted within hours, leaving the boat off station service for less than four hours.

On 8 June 2014 RNLI volunteer and stalwart of the Port Isaac community Bob Bulgin was awarded the British Empire Medal (BEM) in recognition of his contribution to charity at the station's Annual Lifeboat Service. Acting as the Queen's representative, Colonel Edward Bolitho OBE, Lord Lieutenant of Cornwall, presented the medal to Bob in front of fellow RNLI volunteers, family and friends. The service was taken by RNLI Chaplain Father John May, with readings by Colonel Bolitho and Damien Bolton, senior helm. During the service Bob was presented with a BEM medal by the Lord Lieutenant of Cornwall. He had been a volunteer with the station for seventeen years, as Press Officer and also as Chairman of the fundraising branch for more than a decade.

During his time with the RNLI, Bob has organised numerous

balls, auctions, lotteries, clay shoots and tea parties to bring funds into the charity's collection boxes. He also liaises with the local media, and helps to raise the profile of the RNLI's volunteer crew amongst the local community. Bob took a brief moment to say: 'This sort of thing doesn't happen without a great team, and the crew and committee of Port Isaac RNLI are second to none.'

On the same day, three further awards were made by Col Edward Bolitho in company with RNLI Divisional Inspector Tom Mansell. One went to retiring Lifeboat Operations Manager Phil Tidey, who was received a pair of inscribed binoculars together with a framed Certificate of Thanks from the Institution to mark ten years of voluntary service. Two Bronze Badge awards were made to Fundraising Committee members Christine Clifton, the Secretary, and Cheryl Webster, the Assistant Box Secretary.

Between 1967, when the station was reopened, and January 2016, the Port Isaac inshore lifeboats have been launched 652 times on service and saved 336 lives, and the volunteer crews have been involved in some truly outstanding rescues.

Port Isaac's inshore lifeboat Copeland Bell (D-707) was placed on station in November 2009. (Nicholas Leach)

Port Isaac Paintings

ourteen years ago well known local artist Frank McNichol, together with Port Isaac RNLI Chairman Bob Bulgin BEM, set up an arts workshop to encourage local artist development and continue a tradition established by Frank over the previous twenty-seven years of supporting his dedicated charity, the RNLI.

For two years Frank created marine-based lifeboat paintings, donating both the artwork and reproduction rights to Port Isaac RNLI. Two of these can be seen below. These paintings were reproduced as special art editions and Christmas cards and the original paintings put up for the Annual Christmas Lifeboat Draw.

Since then over eight artists have followed Frank's lead, all of which have created very significant funds for the lifeboat thereby continuing a tradition to this very day. This section presents some of these images, with notes relating to the paintings and artists, who have generously donated their artwork to Port Isaac RNLI.

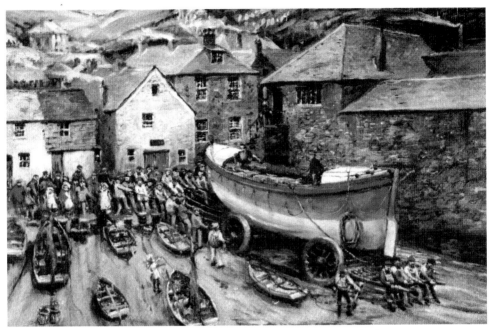

This is the first painting created by Frank McNichol for Port Isaac RNLI and captures the dramatic scene on 9 December 1911 when people from the village turned out to help launch Richard and Sarah (III) when her volunteer crew answered a call to the Breton schooner Berthe Marie.

The second painting created by Frank McNichol shows Richard and Sarah (III) with many of the villagers lending a hand as the lifeboat is hauled back to the original lifeboat house high up on the east side of the village, overlooking the harbour. This scene has been set around the rescue of the fishing boat Flossie and her sole occupant on 14 October 1915, which proved to be the last service undertaken by the station's pulling and sailing lifeboats.

Artist Sian Fletcher has long-standing connections with Port Isaac RNLI. Her husband, two sons and a nephew have all been volunteers on the lifeboat and her husband holds an RNLI letter of appreciation. In this dramatic painting, Sian captured a launch on 20 February 1877 when villagers, crew and horses hauled the lifeboat and carriage overland up steep hills, narrow lanes and across fields, buffeted by driving sleet and howling winds, five miles to Port Quin to launch to the aid of the barque Ada Melmore.

Artist Katie Childs is no stranger to Port Isaac RNLI. Her father, Ted, served on the crew for eleven years, later becoming Honorary Secretary. Katie runs an art gallery at the top of the village and in this oil painting, 'Safe Haven', Katie shows the village covered in snow – a rare occurrence but not unheard of – and with a welcoming glow emanating from the lifeboat house in the centre of the old village.

This evocative painting by Les Henson links with the painting by Frank McNichol of the recovery of the lifeboat (see page 103) following the service to the Breton schooner Berthe Marie. It shows Richard and Sarah (III)'s crew undertaking the arduous row out to the schooner as she lays to her anchors while in imminent danger of running ashore on the rugged coast to the west of Port Isaac harbour.

Roy Ritchie's fairy tale image of Father Christmas setting off from the lifeboat station on his annual delivery mission to the children of North Cornwall captures the festival spirit, and is one of four Christmas themed images Roy has created for Port Isaac RNLI since 2000. Port Isaac RNLI have a dedicated Father Christmas, who has appeared at the station's Christmas fair for the past eighteen years. This has proved a popular image, and cards and special edition prints of it have generated thousands of pounds for RNLI funds.

Artist Caroline Cleave has a close family association with Port Isaac RNLI as she owns, together with her husband Jon, the historic lifeboat house on the east side of the harbour which is now an Art Gallery boutique, which was established as a family business in 1990. Caroline has the opportunity to showcase her eclectic mix of designs and artwork in the building. Jon, an author, has served as Honorary Secretary and a Deputy Launching Authority at the lifeboat station, while their son, George, followed in his great-great-grandfather's footsteps as a volunteer lifeboat man. Caroline's painting 'Safe Home In Port', over laid on a contemporary sheet of Victorian music, shows the lifeboat crew gathered at the station following a successful call to service.

Well known West Country artist Ray Balkwill is an elected Academician of the South West Academy of fine and applied arts and a long-standing supporter of Port Isaac RNLI. Taking a historic photograph of the lifeboat being hauled through the 'narrows' of the village, Ray created this fine mixed media painting of Richard and Sarah (III) on her way back to the old lifeboat station. Note the red woollen hats worn by the lifeboat crew. This image has proved to be one of the most popular in the Port Isaac gallery of lifeboat art and copies have been sold worldwide.

Popular local artist Barbara Hawkins has created stunning action-packed scenes depicting the Port Isaac inshore lifeboat on service. The first (opposite) shows the ILB having just launched, with crew on board, speeding out of the harbour to a 'shout', but within the harbour but soon to face the full Atlantic seas beyond the breakwaters. The second painting (above) shows the ILB returning safely to the harbour slipway, overlooked by the old Methodist Chapel, which is now home to the Pottery Gallery. Apart from Barbara's dedicated support for Port Isaac RNLI, she has strong family links. Her husband Billy having served as a Deputy Launching Authority for many years, and her son-in-law Matt Main, who was awarded the RNLI's Bronze medal for gallantry, is one of the station's helmsmen.

Appendices

A • Pulling and Sailing Lifeboats

Years on station (launches/saved)	Dimensions Type	Cost ON	Year built Builder	Name Donor
10.1869–87 (8/57)	32' x 7'7' Self-righter	£246 —	1869 Forrestt, Limehouse	*Richard and Sarah* Gift of Mr & Mrs Thornton West, Streatham
1887–1905 (9/28)	34' x 7'6' Self-righter	£406 135	1887 Forrestt, Limehouse	*Richard and Sarah* Gift of Mr & Mrs Thornton West, Streatham
1905–27 (10/1)	34' x 7'6' Self-righter	£437 334	1892 Forrestt, Limehouse	*Richard and Sarah* Gift of Mr & Mrs Thornton West, Streatham
1927–5.33 (0/0)	35' x 8'10' Rubie SR	£1974 662	1917 Saunders, Cowes	*Ernest Dresden* Legacy Ernest Dresden, Cavendish Sq, London

B • Inshore lifeboats

Years on station (launches/saved)	ON	Name (if any) Donor	Type Notes
6.1967–1977 (135/41)	D–139	— —	15'3' RFD PB16
3.1978–1988 (126/50)	D–257	— Round Tables of Cornwall and Isles of Scilly	15'3' RFD PB16
15.6.1988–5.1997 (215/63)	D–366	*Peter and Mollie Tabor* Mr and Mrs P. R. Tabor	16'3' Avon EA16
29.5.1997–9.1998 (33/23)	D–517	*Spirit of the PCS RE* Officers and Soldiers of the Royal Logistics Corp with contributions from other regiments	16'3' Avon EA16 Wrecked on service 6.9.1998
6–23.9.1998 (0/0)	D–382	— Gift of Mr D. G. Matkin	16'3' Avon EA16 Temporary duty
23.11.1998–6.1999	D–366	*Peter and Molly Tabor* Mr and Mrs P. R. Tabor	16'3' Avon EA16 Temporary duty
3.6.1999–11.2009 (73/41)	D–546	*Spirit of the PCS RE* Local appeal to replace ILB wrecked in 1998	16'3' Avon EA16
23.11.2009–	D–707	*Copeland Bell* Bude Model Boat Appeal, together with other donations and gifts from Cornwall	4.95m IB1

Relief inhore lifeboats • The following Relief ILBs have served at Port Isaac on temporary duty: D-58 (10/8), D-150 (5/1), D-206 (1/0), D-214 (1/1), D-227 (5/0), D-256 (10/5). D-355 (1/2), D-405 (1/0), D-439 (8/0), D-442 (2/3), D-492 (2/0), D-530 (2/0). The figures in brackets represent launches/lives saved.

C • Pulling lifeboat service summary

Richard and Sarah (first) Lifeboat

1870   Oct 24   Brig *Stephano Grosso*, of Genoa, saved 3

1872   Nov 20   Fishing luggers *Castle* and *J.T.K.*, of Port Isaac, saved boats and 4 men in each 8

1877   Feb 20   Barque *Ada Melmore*, of Maryport, saved 10

1882   Mar 26   Schooner *British Queen*, of Wexford, saved 4

1883   Feb 7   Fishing boats *Charles and John*, *Bell*, *Columbia* and *Little Willie*, of Port Isaac, towed in boats and saved 7
                 Other fishing boats, of Port Isaac, stood by

1886   Oct 14   Steamship *Indus*, of Dundee, saved 25

Richard and Sarah (second) Lifeboat

1890   Nov 7   Schooner *Golden Light*, of Penzance, saved 5

1895   Jan 2   Barque *Antoinette*, of St John's NB, saved 10

1899   Oct 1   Steamship *Lynx*, of Cardiff, saved 7

1902   Nov 24   Six fishing boats, of Port Isaac, assisted to mooring

1903   Sep 11   Brig *L'Union*, of Auray, saved 6
                 Brig *L'Union*, of Auray, replaced crew and assisted to save vessel

1904   Dec 9   Three fishing boats, of Port Isaac, helped to moorings

Richard and Sarah (third) Lifeboat

1911   Dec 7   Schooner *Berthe Marie*, of Brest, landed 4 of crew
           8   Schooner *Berthe Marie*, of Brest, replaced crew and assisted to raise anchor

1913   May 30   Fishing boat *Flossie*, of Port Isaac, stood by until moored

1915   Oct 14   Fishing boat *Flossie*, of Port Isaac, saved boat and 1

Edward Dresden Lifeboat

          No services

The only former Port Isaac lifeboat surviving from the pulling and sailing era is Ernest Dresden. After being sold out of service in 1933, she was converted into a motor boat and renamed Courtown. She gradually deteriorated until 2001, when Simon Evans, owner of numerous former lifeboats, acquired her. He took her to his boatyard at St Denis Les Sens in France, where she is pictured, and restored her to her lifeboat appearance. He later moved her, along with all his other lifeboats, to Migennes. (Nicholas Leach)

D • Inshore lifeboat service summary

1967　May 9　Fishing boat *Justine*, saved boat and 1
　　　July 24　Motor launch, saved launch
　　　Aug 15　Two dinghies, saved dinghies and 2
　　　Sep 2　Person washed into the sea, saved 1
1969　June 7　Boy fallen from cliff, recovered a body
　　　July 7　Yacht *Minoru*, stood by
　　　Aug 7　Motor boat, saved boat and 5
　　　22　Motor cruiser *Mervic*, stood by, gave help
　　　Sep 2　Dinghy, gave help
　　　Oct 9　Bather, gave help
1970　May 3　Boys stranded on cliff, stood by
　　　June 8　Yacht *Pat*, saved yacht and 1
　　　Aug 19　Sailing dinghy, saved dinghy and 1
　　　29　Man fallen from rocks, ld an injured man
1971　June 8　Persons stranded on rocks, saved 3
　　　29　Fishing boat *Jan D*, gave help
　　　July 7　Rubber dinghy, escorted
　　　10　Boy fallen from cliff, saved 1
　　　17　Persons stranded on a cliff, stood by
　　　26　Person fallen from cliff, landed 1
　　　27　Persons stranded on a cliff, assisted to save 1
　　　Aug 2　Person fallen from rocks, landed 1
　　　17　Rubber dinghy, saved 2
　　　23　Woman fallen over cliff, landed 1
　　　Sep 7　Persons cut off by the tide, saved 2
　　　17　Man cut off by the tide, saved 7
　　　　　Motor boat, saved boat and 2
1972　Apr 8　Boy fallen from cliff, stood by
　　　13　Man fallen from cliff, stood by
　　　June 11　Cabin cruiser *Viking*, gave help
　　　Aug 6　Motor boat, saved boat and 1
　　　　　Sailing dinghy, escorted
　　　21　Fishing boat *Hettie*, saved boat and 2
1973　May 26　Woman fallen from cliff, gave help
　　　June 17　Outboard dinghy, saved dinghy and 5
　　　24　Persons trapped under cliff, saved 2
　　　26　Person fallen from cliff, saved 1
　　　July 1　Two canoes, saved canoes and 2
　　　25　Two bathers, saved 2
　　　Aug 15　Rubber dinghy, saved dinghy and 2
1974　Aug 15　Persons cut off by the tide, saved 2
　　　16　Motor boat, escorted
　　　22　Persons stranded on cliff, stood by
　　　Sep 16　Outboard dinghy, landed 2
1975　Aug 21　Dinghy, gave help
　　　Oct 5　Cattle fallen from cliff, stood by
1976　May 30　Dory *Yukkie*, saved dory and 2
　　　July 26　Persons cut off by the tide, saved 5
　　　Aug 10　Persons stranded on cliff, gave help
　　　18　Dinghy, saved 1

　　　21　Conveyed a sick person from Bossiney to Boscastle
　　　25　Persons cut off by the tide, landed 2
1977　May 4　Man fallen from cliff, saved 1
　　　July 14　Three persons stranded on cliffs, gave help
　　　17　Skin diver, saved 1
　　　30　Boy fallen from cliff, stood by
　　　31　Man stranded on a cliff, landed 1
　　　Aug 10　Dory, gave help
　　　15　Woman fallen from cliff, gave help
1978　Apr 9　Dory *Thumper*, gave help
　　　May 27　Rubber dinghy, saved dinghy
　　　　　Yacht *Y Ddraig*, escorted
　　　July 16　Dinghy, saved dinghy and 2
　　　Aug 3　Dory, saved dory and 4
　　　11　Sailing dinghy, gave help
　　　14　Two persons in the sea, saved 1
　　　18　Recovered the body of a bather
　　　25　Landed a body from the foot of cliffs
　　　Sep 4　Man cut off by the tide, saved 1
1979　Apr 16　Took an injured man from Epphaven to Port Isaac
　　　17　Yacht *Midnight Mint*, gave help
　　　May 9　Two persons stranded on a cliff, gave help
　　　July 8　Fishing boat *Haranna*, landed 3 and stood by
　　　9　Landed a body from the sea
　　　　　Landed the body of a swimmer
　　　30　Sailing dinghy, saved dinghy and 1
　　　Aug 7　Persons cut off by the tide, saved 4
　　　26　Dinghy, gave help
　　　Sep 2　Yacht, saved yacht and 2
　　　29　Sailing dinghy, escorted dinghy
1980　May 12　Dinghy *Sylvan*, saved dinghy and 3
　　　July 5　Bather, landed a body
　　　27　Woman fallen from cliff, stood by
　　　28　Two rubber dinghies, saved 4
　　　Aug 3　Motor boat *Little Lisa*, saved 2
　　　26　A youth fallen from a cliff, gave help
1981　July 12　Youth stranded on cliff, gave help
　　　Aug 13　Persons cut off by the tide, gave help
　　　Sep 18　Sailboards, landed 3
1982　Apr 25　Person cut off by the tide, saved 1
1983　Aug 17　Sailing dinghy, saved boat and 1
　　　　　Sailing dinghies, gave help
　　　26　Two persons in the sea, saved 2
　　　　　Two persons cut off by the tide, saved 2
1984　Apr 21　Injured man at foot of cliff, gave help
　　　May 7　Sailing dinghy, saved dinghy and 2
　　　June 30　Speedboat, saved boat and 3

	July 14	Two bathers, stood by
	Aug 24	Four persons cut off by the tide, gave help
1985	June 29	Motor boat, saved boat and 3
1986	May 1	Sailing dinghy, saved dinghy and 2
	4	Two sailboards, saved two boards and 2
	Aug 23	Rubber dinghy, gave help
	25	Sailboard, saved board and 1
		Sailing dinghy, stood by
	June 12	Body in water, gave help
	July 10	Swimmers, landed 2
	20	Sailboard, saved board and 1
	22	Club rescue boat, escorted
	Aug 8	Persons cut off by the tide, saved 2
	Sep 6	Person fallen from cliff, landed body
	22	Sailboard, stood by
1988	Apr 3	Person in difficulty, stood by
		Person fallen from cliff, saved 1
	5	Person in difficulty, stood by
	June 4	Motor boat, saved boat and 1
	July 1	Sailboard, stood by
	Aug 8	Rowing boat, saved 1
		Sailing dinghy, saved dinghy and 2
	28	Animal, gave help
	Sep 11	Persons cut off by the tide, stood by
	Oct 16	Person in difficulty, stood by
1989	Apr 22	Small motor boat, craft brought in
	May 29	Small powered boat with cabin, craft brought in
	June 18	Sailboard, saved craft and 1
	July 4	Person cut off by tide, saved 2
	July 18	Injured person fallen from cliff, gave help
	26	Sail yacht with aux engine, stood by
	Aug 27	Sailboard, saved craft and 2
	31	Person cut off by tide, saved 1
	Sep 17	Rowing boat, saved craft
	18	Sailboard, saved craft
1990	July 19	Person cut off by tide, saved 5
	July 22	Injured person fallen from cliff, stood by
	29	Sailboard, saved craft and 1
	Aug 11	Sailboard, saved craft and 1
	26	Injured person fallen from cliff, gave help
	Sep 23	Sailboard, saved craft and 1
1991	Mar 14	Person cut off by tide, saved 2
	30	Person cut off by tide, saved 2
	Apr 1	Sailboard, saved craft and 1
	20	Sailboard, saved craft and 1
	July 6	Sailboard, saved craft and 2
	9	Person cut off by tide, gave help
	10	Person cut off by tide, gave help
	17	Injured person fallen from cliff, stood by
	26	Injured person fallen from cliff, gave help
	28	Person cut off by tide, stood by

	Aug 21	Sailboard, craft brought in
	26	Inflatable dinghy, craft brought in
	29	Sailboard, craft saved
	31	Swimmers, landed 3
	Sep 9	Person stranded, gave help
	Oct 21	Sailboard, saved 1
1992	Apr 18	Sailboard, saved craft and 1
	May 17	Small open powered boat, craft brought in
	June 4	Person fallen from cliff, gave help
	18	Sailboard, saved craft and 2
	July 11	Sail yacht with aux engine, stood by
	15	Recovery of dead body, landed a body
	20	Fishing vessel, craft brought in
	30	Canoe, escorted
	Aug 9	Injured person fallen from cliff, gave help
	16	Ill crewman on rowing boat, landed 1
	29	Sail catamaran, saved craft and 1
	Oct 27	Animal, gave help
1993	May 2	Person in danger of being carried away by tide, stood by
	20	Small open powered boat, craft brought in
	June 26	Sail multihull, landed 1 and saved craft
	Aug 5	Person cut off by tide, saved 1
	22	Sailboard, craft saved
	22	Sailboard, saved craft and 2
	29	Sail yacht with aux engine, gave help
	29	Small open powered boat, craft brought in
	Sep 4	Person fallen from cliff, landed a body
	19	Sailboard, saved 1
1994	May 5	Fishing vessel *Bethany May*, two persons and craft brought in
	June 28	Motor cruiser *Avanti*, saved boat and 2
	July 11	Sailing dinghy *Epic*, escorted boat
	24	Three swimmers, landed 1
	30	Man fallen from cliff, recovered a body
	Aug 6	Motor boat, two persons & craft brought in
	16	Rubber dinghy *Drifter*, five persons and craft brought in
	Oct 2	Two dogs, saved two dogs
1995	Apr 29	Man fallen from cliffs, saved 1
	May 6	Woman fallen from cliffs onto beach, stood by
	May 27	Dog, gave help
	June 23	Woman stranded on cliff, stood by
	24	Sail training vessel *Maria Asumpta*, landed two bodies
	July 8	Woman fallen from cliff, gave help
	15	Man stranded on cliff, gave help
		Yacht, gave help
	31	Injured youth at Tregardock Beach, injured youth brought in

	Aug 15	Yacht *Harry O*, three persons and craft brought in
	21	Sheep fallen from cliff, saved sheep
	Sep 10	Fishing vessel *Mako III*, gave help
1996	July 15	Man stranded on rocks at Tintagel Castle, stood by
	29	Two rubber dinghies, landed 2 and two craft brought in
	Aug 4	Bomb on Pine Avon Beach, gave help
	27	Canoe, escorted craft
	Oct 27	Two men cut off by tide, saved 2
1997	Apr 20	Two divers, gave help
		Man cut off by tide at Castle Rock, landed 1
	May 11	Rock ILB D-489, four people and craft brought in
	12	Dog stranded on rocks, gave help
	22	Ordnance in sea, took out bomb disposal personnel
	June 5	Missing diver, landed 1
	Aug 7	Man fallen from cliffs, gave help
	16	Five youths cut off by tide, landed 2 and saved 3
	Sep 1	Three surfboards, landed 1 and three boards brought in
	18	Surfboard, landed 1 and board brought in
	20	Diver support craft *Rubber Glove*, landed 2 and saved craft
	Oct 4	Missing woman, landed a body
1998	Mar 3	Man stranded on breakwater, landed 1
	19	Body in sea, landed a body
	Apr 14	Dog in sea, gave help
	May 1	Youth fallen over cliffs at Ocean View caravan park, assisted to save 1
	June 22	Fishing vessel *Flying Fish*, saved 1
	July 22	Diver, gave help
	Aug 4	Body board, saved 1
	11	Surf board, landed 1 and craft brought in
		Swimmer, one person brought in
	16	Diver support craft Bude Divers, six people and craft brought in
	30	Inflatable dinghy, saved craft
		Diver support craft, gave help
	Sep 6	Man and boy trapped in a cave at Bossiney, gave help
1999	Mar 28	Two people stranded on cliff, stood by
	May 22	Inflatable dinghy, gave help
	Aug 31	Divers, landed 2
2000		No effective services
2001	Feb 19	Dog fallen over cliff, gave help
	June 1	Missing person, gave help
		Search for casualty's clothing, gave help
	16	Canoes, saved two craft
	Aug 10	Life raft, craft brought in
	26	Fishing boat *Orcades II*, gave help - crew gave medical assistance
2002	Jan 4	Dog fallen over cliff, gave help - saved dog
	Apr 22	Deer fallen from cliff, gave help
	Aug 27	Dive support RIB, two people and craft brought in
	Sep 24	Person injured on cliff, stood by
	Oct 2	Motor boat *Dabbler*, two people and craft brought in
2003	Mar 22	Motor boat, escorted casualty
	Apr 18	Surfer, landed 1 and craft brought in
		People on breakwater, landed 2
	Aug 26	Person in danger of drowning, landed 1
2004	May 16	Diver, landed 1
	19	Person and dog cut off by tide, gave help – located casualty and directed helicopter
	June 1	People in the sea, landed 1
	Aug 16	Bude inshore lifeboat, three people and craft brought in
2005	May 30	Canoe, landed 1 and canoe brought in
	June 2	Motor boat, one person and craft brought in
	12	Powered boat, three people and craft brought in
	July 25	Canoe, saved 1
2006	Feb 5	Motor boat, one person and craft brought in
	Mar 29	Surfers, two people brought in
	Apr 9	Fishing vessel *Mary D*, gave help
	28	Powered boat, escorted casualty
	30	Diver, gave help - assisted helicopter winchman
	May 13	Surfboarders, two people brought in
	June 14	Person on rocks, landed 1
	July 28	Powered boat *Three Jays*, four people and craft brought in
	Aug 7	Missing person, landed a body
	8	Dog, gave help - brought in dog
	Sep 14	Canoe two people and craft brought in
2007	June 1	People in the sea, landed 1
	16	Injured person on rocks, one person brought in
2008	July 23	Marine debris, gave help
	29	Canoe, craft brought in and saved 2
	Dec 27	Surfboards, stood by
2009	Jan 10	People cut off by tide, stood by
	Apr 5	Surfers, stood by
	July 15	Person on rocks, landed 1
	25	Tender to yacht *Lady of Rudding*, craft brought in
	Sep 12	Kayak, craft brought in and saved 1

	Oct 2	People in the sea, two people brought in
	13	People cut off by tide, three people brought in
	Dec 30	Dog, two people brought in and recovered dog
2010	Mar 14	Metal container, gave help
	June 3	Angling vessel *Dylan*, one person and craft brought in
	July 12	Human body, landed a body
	Aug 14	People stranded on breakwater, landed 2
2011	Feb 20	Rowing boat *Corsair*, saved 7
	Apr 6	Powered boat, two people brought in
	7	Kayak, people landed 2
	June 1	Surfboard, one person and surfboard brought in
	Sep 1	People cut off by tide, landed 2
2012	Jan 1	Person in the water, saved 1
	Mar 25	Powered boat, rendered assistance
	Apr 8	Person in water, gave help and saved 1
	12	Animal, rendered assistance
	26	Animal, rendered assistance

	May 26	Person on cliff, 2 people assisted
	June 4	Person on island, 1 person assisted
	July 21	Animal, rendered assistance
	Aug 11	Fishing vessel, 2 persons and craft brought in
	Dec 31	Person in water, gave help and saved 1
2013	Aug 6	Person on cliff, rendered assistance
	23	Person on cliff, 1 person assisted
2014	Apr 13	Canoe, gave help and 2 people assisted
	Aug 15	Powered boat *Storming*, rendered assistance and 4 people rescued
2015	Apr 16	Dog, rendered assistance
	20	Person on manmade structure, rendered assistance and saved 1
	July 9	Dog, rendered assistance
	Sep 28	Person on rocks, 1 person assisted

Only effective services are included in this listing.

E • Personnel summary

Honorary Secretaries

Frederick Trevan	1869 – 1881
William Guy	1881 – 1883
Rev John Lock	1883 – 1887
Dr M. Trevan, RN	1887 – 1889
William R Guy	1890 – 1893
R. Julyan George	1893 – 1911
Dr W. Roy Jackson	1911 – 1923
R.Y.H. Christmas, MRCS	1923 – 1933
Raymond 'Boss' Harris	1967 – 1975
David Castle	1975 – 1995
Jon Cleave	1.1 – 17.6.1996
Edward 'Ted' Childs	6.1996 – 1999
Jon Cleave	1999 – 2000
Robert Monk	2000 – 2003
Philip Tidey	2004 – 2014
Chris Bolton	2014 –

Medical Officers

Dr William Baird	1967 – 1981
Dr James Lunny	1982 – 2008
Dr Alan Sainsbury	2009 –
Dr Sandra Barfield	2009 –

Station Chaplain

Reverend Dr Elizabeth Wild

Station and Branch Treasurer

David Raynor

Coxswains

James Haynes*	1869-95
John Haynes	1895-1908
Thomas Mitchell Collins	1908-10
Joseph Honey	1910-20
William Harris Steer	1920-31
George Honey	1931-33

*Cox James Haynes was awarded a Silver medal on 12 December 1895 in recognition of his good services for many years.

Helms

No records prior to 1980; since 1980 the following qualified and trained as helms, and became senior helms:

Neville Andrews
Mark Provis
Andy Walton
Kevin Dingle
Steve Taylor
Richard Hambly

Helms in 2016 are:
Damien Bolton (Senior Helmsman since 2011)
Andy Cameron
Matt Main
Del Allerton-Baldwin

Service Awards

Medals for rescues have been awarded as follows:

Silver Medals
William Mitchell : 5 October 1859
William Mitchell : 24 October 1870
James Haines : 12 December 1895
Damien Bolton : 8 April 2012

Bronze Medals
Matt Main : 8 April 2012
Nicki Bradbury : 8 April 2012

Honorary Awards

Honorary awards recognise exemplary service to the RNLI. Details of badge awards before 1985 are not available. The following awards have been made since then:

Kathleen Castle : Gold Badge, circa 1985
George Moth : Gold Badge, April 1989
David Castle : Silver Badge and Gold Badge
Molly Farmer : Silver Badge, circa 1994
Between 1994 and 2016 these awards were made:
Bronze badges to Jan Rowe, Liz Bolton, Pat Pearson, David Raynor, Cheryl Webster and Chris Clifton
Bronze and Silver Badges to Annie Price, Bob Bulgin, Carole Raynor and Sandie Bulgin
Gold badges were awarded to Bob Bulgin BEM and David Raynor, January 2016

F • Lifeboat station personnel 2016

LB OPERATIONS MANAGER

Chris Bolton (Photo Tony Barnes)
Holiday Provider

DEPUTY LAUNCHING AUTH

Phil Tidey
Engineer

DEPUTY LAUNCHING AUTH

John Brown
Retired fisherman

DEPUTY LAUNCHING AUTH

John Collins, Deputy Launching
Authority, Fish Trader

DEPUTY LAUNCHING AUTH

Nigel Sherratt
Electrical Engineer

DEPUTY LAUNCHING AUTH

Richard Hambly
Paramedic

CHAIRMAN & PRESS OFF'R

Bob Bulgin
Retired Company Director

DEPUTY PRESS OFFICER

Faye Archell
Teacher

TREASURER

David Raynor
Electronics Engineer

G • Lifeboat crew 2016

SENIOR HELMSMAN

Damien Bolton, Clinical lead for
Orthopaedic Trauma

HELMSMAN

Andy Cameron
Surf Company Owner

HELMSMAN

Matt Main
Restaurateur/photographer

HELMSMAN

Del Alerton-Baldwin
Policeman

CREW MEMBER

Nicola Bradbury
Cornish Pasty Shop owner

CREW MEMBER

Kevin Dingle
Builder

CREW MEMBER

Ian Johnson, Pharmaceutical sales
account manager

CREW MEMBER

Mark Grills
Builder

CREW MEMBER

Tom Brown
Fisherman

CREW MEMBER

Darren Milner
Plumber

CREW MEMBER

Andy Hallam
Builder

CREW MEMBER

James Bolton
Consultancy

CREW MEMBER

George Cleave
Fish Merchant

CREW MEMBER

Jon Wild
Brewer

CREW MEMBER

Richard Watson
Boatbuilder

CREW MEMBER

Harry Hambly
Student

CREW MEMBER

Jack Greenhaigh
Student

SHORE WORKER

Trevor Beare,
Marine Engineer, Shore Works

D-707 Copeland Bell cutting throug[h] the gut at Port Gaverne with the thre[e] crew members on board wo receiv[ed] gallantry medals. (Mike Lavis/RNL[I])